ROAD

To get your ebook, go to
www.tincanknits.com/redeem
and enter this code:

RW99AHGY

by Alexa Ludeman and Emily Wessel
Tin Can Knits | **www.tincanknits.com**
Vancouver, Canada and Edinburgh, UK

CONTENTS

ROAD TRIP

14 knits inspired by the open road

Whether setting out on a solo journey, cuddling up on a romantic weekend, or recreating the camping trips of your childhood, a road trip is a special kind of getaway. The open road holds a romance for young folk seeking adventure, couples searching for that perfect picnic spot, and families who visit their favourite places year after year.

With the routines of home far behind, easy conversations lead to big dreams. You return home with fresh enthusiasm and energy. Relaxing evenings around the campfire are the perfect time to enjoy food and chat with old friends and new loves. Your traditional stopping places, seen again through a child's eyes, seem exciting and new. The road holds untold adventures, you never know what you might find around the bend.

These nostalgic knits are inspired by our trips across Canada: expansive views from mountain passes, coffee stops in quaint towns, and bonfires on remote beaches. Along with the patterns we have shared photos and stories from some of our favourite places and road trip memories. With cables, colourwork and lace, this collection is full of delicious knits. Pack up your needles and yarn and head out on the open road today!

ROAD TRIP 1

Alexa Ludeman ✦ Emily Wessel

Young or old, the open road beckons to the adventurous spirit in all of us. When I was nineteen, I packed up all my worldly possessions and took a bus across the continent from Toronto to San Francisco. This epic solo road trip took me through foreign landscapes to an exciting new city. In a time before cell phones and constant communication I was genuinely alone out in the unknown world. This was a journey of growing up and finding myself, and it all began with a road trip.

Hitting the road, you are untethered from routine. Leaving your regular life behind you see the world and your place in it afresh. Under wide open skies you can dream big, make plans, and try new things.

So if you are feeling hemmed in, uncertain, or uninspired, perhaps it is time to set off on an adventure of your own, and see what there is to see around the next bend in the road.

~ Emily

"THE OPEN ROAD

CLAYOQUOT

geometric Fair Isle *by Alexa Ludeman*

At Canada's far western edge is a wild place called Clayoquot Sound. Old-growth rainforests plunge down steep sided islands into the cold and vibrant waters of the Pacific. Fog, wind, and stormy weather make this landscape inhospitable for most of the year. But when summer light sparkles on these jewelled waters, people come to kayak, camp, and fish in this pristine wild wonderland.

materials:

Yarn: DK weight yarn in 3 colours - see table for yardage *(samples shown in **Sweet Fiber Merino Twist DK** in 'winter', 'moss', 'marshland', 'paper birch', and 'something blue')*

Needles: US #4 / 3.5mm and US #6 / 4mm *(or as req'd to meet gauge)* 16-47" circular needle and DPNs in each size

Gauge: 22 sts & 28 rounds / 4" in stockinette on larger needles

Notions: stitch markers, darning needle, 5-13 1/2" buttons

Alexa Ludeman ✦ Emily Wessel

sizing: Pattern includes 7 child and 10 adult sizes.

Note: table lists finished garment measurements. Choose a size based on your chest / bust measurement + desired ease.

Size	Chest	Sleeve	Hem to Under-arm	Upper Arm	Yardage	
					MC	CC1 / CC2
0-6 mo	18"	6.5"	6"	6"	300	50 / 25
6-12 mo	20"	7.5"	6.5"	6.5"	340	60 / 30
1-2 yrs	22"	8.5"	8"	7"	380	70 / 35
2-4 yrs	24"	10.5"	9"	7.75"	450	90 / 45
4-6 yrs	26"	12"	10"	8"	550	100 / 50
6-8 yrs	27.5"	13"	13"	8.75"	750	110 / 55
8-10 yrs	29"	14"	15"	9"	850	120 / 60
XS	31"	17"	15"	9.75"	950	140 / 70
S	33"	18"	16"	10"	1100	160 / 80
SM	35"	18"	16"	10.5"	1200	170 / 85
M	37"	19"	17"	11.25"	1300	190 / 95
ML	39"	19"	17"	12"	1400	200 / 100
L	41"	20"	18"	13"	1500	210 / 105
XL	44"	20"	18"	14"	1600	220 / 110
XXL	48"	20"	19"	15"	1750	260 / 130
3XL	52"	21"	19"	16.5"	1900	300 / 150
4XL	58"	21"	20"	18.5"	2200	330 / 165

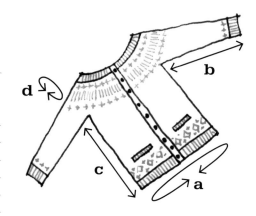

a chest / bust
b sleeve
c hem to underarm
d upper arm

sizing notes: This cardi looks best with 0-1" positive ease. Emily (35" bust) is wearing size SM with 0" ease, Hunter is wearing 2-4 yrs with 1" positive ease.

pattern:

This cardigan is knit seamlessly from the bottom up. First the body and sleeves are worked separately, then they are joined together and the yoke is worked. The body is steeked at centre front and button bands are worked last.

sleeves: *(make 2 the same)*

Sleeves are worked in the round from cuff to underarm. With smaller needles and MC cast on 32 (32, 32, 36, 36, 40, 40, **44, 44, 44, 48, 48, 52, 52, 56, 60, 60**) sts, PM and join for working in the round.

Work in 2x2 ribbing (*k2, p2*) for 1.5 (**2**) inches for child (**adult**) sizes. Change to larger needles and knit 2 rounds.

Work rounds 1-3 of chart A. Knit 2 rounds in MC.

Inc round: k1, m1, knit to last st, m1, k1
[2 sts inc]
Knit 6 (6, 6, 6, 6, 6, 6, **6, 6, 6, 6, 6, 5, 5, 5, 4, 4**) rounds.

Work these last 7 (7, 7, 7, 7, 7, 7, **7, 7, 7, 7, 7, 6, 6, 6, 5, 5**) rounds a total of 1 (2, 3, 3, 4, 4, 5, **5, 6, 7, 7, 9, 10, 13, 13, 15, 21**) times. [34 (36, 38, 42, 44, 48, 50, **54, 56, 58, 62, 66, 72, 78, 82, 90, 102**) sts]

Continue knitting each round until sleeve measures 6.5 (7.5, 8.5, 10.5, 12, 13, 14, **17, 18, 18, 19, 19, 20, 20, 20, 21, 21**) inches (*or desired length to underarm*).

Knit 3 (3, 3, 3, 3, 3, 3, **4, 4, 4, 4, 5, 5, 5, 6, 6, 6**) sts, then place the last 6 (6, 6, 6, 6, 6, 6, **8, 8, 8, 8, 10, 10, 10, 12, 12, 12**) sts worked on hold for underarm, then place the remaining sts on hold separately. *Tip: when breaking yarn leave a 12 inch tail to graft underarm stitches later.*

pockets: *(make 2 the same)*

With larger needles and MC cast on 14 (16, 18, 20, 22, 24, 24, **28, 28, 30, 30, 30, 30, 32, 32, 32, 32**) sts.

Work in stockinette *(knit 1 row, purl 1 row)* until piece measures 2 (2, 3, 3, 3, 3, 4, **4, 4, 4, 5, 5, 5, 5, 5, 5, 5**) inches from cast on. Place sts on hold.

body:

The body is worked in the round, then steeked at centre front to become a cardigan. The first 5 stitches of the round are the steek stitches. All stitches, apart from charted rounds, are worked in MC.

Using smaller needles and MC cast on 99 (111, 123, 131, 143, 151, 159, **167, 183, 191, 207, 215, 223, 239, 263, 287, 319**) sts, PM, and join for working in the round.

Set up round: k5, PM, [k2, p2] to the last 2 sts, k2

Work as established *(knitting your knits and purling your purls)* until ribbing measures 1.5 (**2**) inches from cast on for child (**adult**) sizes. Change to larger needles.

Next round: k6, m1, knit to end
[100 (112, 124, 132, 144, 152, 160, **168, 184, 192, 208, 216, 224, 240, 264, 288, 320**) sts]

Child sizes: knit 4 rounds
Adult sizes: knit 6 rounds

Sizes 0-6 mo to 4-6 yrs: work rounds 1-3 of chart B
Sizes 6-8 yrs to 4XL: work rounds 1-13 of chart C

All sizes: Using MC, knit one round.

Decrease round: k5, knit, decreasing 0 (0, 2, 0, 0, 0, 0, **0, 4, 0, 6, 0, 0, 0, 4, 4, 4**) sts evenly to end
[100 (112, 122, 132, 144, 152, 160, **168, 180, 192, 202, 216, 224, 240, 260, 284, 316**) sts]

Knit every round until body measures 3.5 (3.5, 4.5, 4.5, 4.5, 4.5, 5.5, **6, 6, 6, 7, 7, 7, 7, 7, 7, 7**) inches from cast on.

insert pockets:

Round 1: knit to marker, k4 (4, 4, 4, 5, 5, 5, **5, 5, 6, 6, 8, 8, 10, 10, 12, 12**), PM, [k1, p1] 7 (8, 9, 10, 11, 12, 12, **14, 14, 15, 15, 15, 15, 16, 16, 16, 16**) times, PM, knit to last 18 (20, 22, 24, 27, 29, 29, **33, 33, 36, 36, 38, 38, 42, 42, 44, 44**) sts, PM, [p1, k1] 7 (8, 9, 10, 11, 12, 12, **14, 14, 15, 15, 15, 15, 16, 16, 16, 16**) times, PM, knit to end
Round 2: knit to second marker, rib to marker as established, knit to marker, rib to marker as established, knit to end

chart A: work rounds 1-3

3
2
1

|4 st rep|

chart B: work rounds 1-3

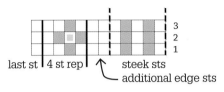

3
2
1

last st | 4 st rep | ↑ steek sts
additional edge sts

chart C: work rounds 1-13

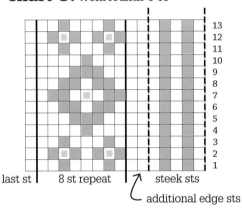

13
12
11
10
9
8
7
6
5
4
3
2
1

last st | 8 st repeat | ↑ steek sts
additional edge sts

chart D: work rounds 1-9

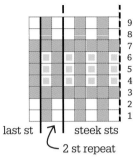

9
8
7
6
5
4
3
2
1

last st ↑ steek sts
2 st repeat

chart E: work rounds 1-13

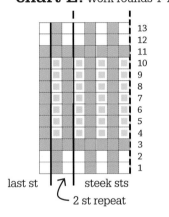

13
12
11
10
9
8
7
6
5
4
3
2
1

last st ↑ steek sts
2 st repeat

key & abbreviations:

☐ **MC** - knit with main colour

▨ **CC1** - knit with contrast colour 1

▨ **CC2** - knit with contrast colour 2

chart notes:

Charts are read from right to left, all sts are knit.

The first 5 stitches of charts B, C, D, E, and F are the sts between the BOR marker and the first marker; these sts are at centre front and will be 'used up' when the steek is cut. The dotted lines indicate the marker locations.

For charts B, C, D, E, and F, work the steek stitches, then any additional edge stitches, then repeat the stitch repeat shown as many times as possible, to the last edge stitch.

chart F: work rounds 1-17

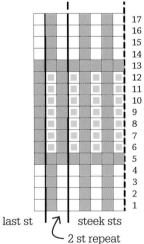

17
16
15
14
13
12
11
10
9
8
7
6
5
4
3
2
1

last st ↑ steek sts
2 st repeat

Repeat round 2 until pocket ribbing measures 0.75 (**1**) inches for child (**adult**) sizes.

Next round: knit to second marker, bind off 14 (16, 18, 20, 22, 24, 24, **28, 28, 30, 30, 30, 30, 32, 32, 32, 32**) sts, knit to next marker, bind off same number again, knit to end.

Place held sts from pockets onto a spare needle.

Next round: knit to bound off sts, knit across held sts from pocket, knit to second set of bound off sts, knit across held sts from second pocket, knit to end.

The pockets are now incorporated into the body of the sweater. The sides and bottom of the pocket will be sewn down later.

Using MC, knit every round until body measures 6 (6.5, 8, 9, 10, 13, 15, **15, 16, 16, 17, 17, 18, 18, 19, 19, 20**) inches from cast on (*or desired length to underarm*).

join sleeves and body:

Knit 5 sts *(steek)*, knit 21 (24, 27, 29, 32, 34, 36, **37, 40, 43, 45, 48, 50, 54, 58, 64, 72**) sts *(right front)*, place the next 6 (6, 6, 6, 6, 6, 6, **8, 8, 8, 8, 10, 10, 10, 12, 12, 12**) sts on hold for right underarm.

Knit across 28 (30, 32, 36, 38, 42, 44, **46, 48, 50, 54, 56, 62, 68, 70, 78, 90**) held sts from right sleeve *(all except the underarm sts)*.

Knit 41 (47, 51, 57, 63, 67, 71, **73, 79, 85, 91, 95, 99, 107, 115, 127, 143**) body sts *(back)*, place the next 6 (6, 6, 6, 6, 6, 6, **8, 8, 8, 8, 10, 10, 10, 12, 12, 12**) sts on hold for left underarm.

Knit across held sts from left sleeve as at right. Knit across remaining sts to end *(left front)*.

[144 (160, 174, 192, 208, 224, 236, **244, 260, 276, 294, 308, 328, 356, 376, 416, 472**) yoke sts]

yoke:

Knit 2 (2, 2, 2, 6, 8, 3, **3, 5, 8, 11, 15, 15, 19, 19, 23, 23**) rounds.

Next round: knit to marker, knit, decreasing 0 (0, 2, 0, 0, 0, 4, **4, 4, 4, 6, 4, 0, 4, 0, 0, 0**) sts evenly [144 (160, 172, 192, 208, 224, 232, **240, 256, 272, 288, 304, 328, 352, 376, 416, 472**) sts]

first yoke chart:

Sizes 0-6 mo to 6-8 yrs: work rounds 1-3 of chart B.
Sizes 8-10 yrs to 4XL: work rounds 1-13 of chart C.

All sizes: knit 1 round in MC.

Next round: knit to marker, [k6, k2tog] to last 11 (11, 7, 11, 11, 11, 3, **11, 11, 11, 11, 11, 3, 11, 3, 11, 3**) sts, knit to end [128 (142, 152, 170, 184, 198, 204, **212, 226, 240, 254, 268, 288, 310, 330, 366, 414**) sts]

Knit 1 round in MC.

second yoke chart:

Sizes 0-6 mo to 1-2 yrs: Work rounds 1-9 of chart D.
Sizes 2-4 yrs to XS: Work rounds 1-13 of chart E.
Sizes S to 4XL: Work rounds 1-17 of chart F.

All sizes: knit 1 round in MC.

Next round: knit to marker, [k1, k2tog] to last 3 (11, 3, 3, 11, 7, 7, **3, 11, 7, 3, 11, 7, 11, 7, 7, 7**) sts, knit to end [88 (100, 104, 116, 128, 136, 140, **144, 156, 164, 172, 184, 196, 212, 224, 248, 280**) sts]

Knit 1 round in MC.

third yoke chart:

All sizes: Work rounds 1-3 of chart B.
Knit 1 round in MC.

Sizes 0-6 mo to 2-4 yrs: knit to marker, [k6, k2tog] to last 3 (7, 3, 7) sts, knit to end
Sizes 4-6 yrs to adult S: knit to marker, [k2, k2tog] to last 3 sts, knit to end
Sizes SM to L: knit to marker, [k1, k2tog] to last 0 (**2, 2, 2**) sts, knit to end
Sizes XL, XXL: knit to marker, [k1, k2tog, k2tog] to last **2 (4**) sts, knit to end
Sizes 3XL, 4XL: knit to marker, [k2tog] to last st, k1 [78 (89, 92, 103, 98, 104, 107, **110, 119, 111, 117, 125, 133, 130, 138, 127, 143**) sts]

All sizes: knit 1 round.

Next round: knit to marker, knit, decreasing 7 (14, 9, 16, 11, 9, 12, **15, 20, 12, 14, 18, 22, 15, 19, 8, 24**) sts evenly to end [71 (75, 83, 87, 87, 95, 95, **95, 99, 99, 103, 107, 111, 115, 119, 119, 119**) sts]

Alexa Ludeman ✦ Emily Wessel

short row back-of-neck shaping:

Short row shaping raises the back of neck relative to the front, for a more comfortable fit. *You may choose to omit this section.*

Set up round: knit to marker, k22 (23, 26, 27, 27, 30, 30, **30, 31, 31, 33, 34, 35, 37, 38, 38, 38**), PM, k22 (24, 26, 28, 28, 30, 30, **30, 32, 32, 32, 34, 36, 36, 38, 38, 38**), PM, knit to end

Short row 1 (RS): knit to 3 sts before 3rd marker, w&t
Short row 2 (WS): purl to 3 sts before next marker, w&t
Short row 3: knit to 4 sts before wrapped st, w&t
Short row 4: purl to 4 sts before wrapped st, w&t
Repeat short rows 3-4 an additional 0 (0, 1, 1, 1, 1, 1, **2, 2, 2, 2, 3, 3, 3, 3, 3, 3**) times.

Knit to end of round, picking up wraps and knitting them together with the sts they wrap. Then knit one complete round, picking up remaining wraps and knitting them together with the sts they wrap.

collar:

Switch to smaller needles and remove all markers.

Ribbing: knit to marker, [k2, p2] to last 2 sts, k2
Work as established until ribbing measures 1 (**1.25**) inches for child (**adult**) sizes. Bind off.

steek cardigan:

Before steeking, wet block your garment to even out the Fair Isle sections *(add white vinegar to the water to prevent colours from bleeding)*.

The first 5 sts of the round are the steek stitches. You will cut up the centre of these stitches to open the cardigan at centre front. First reinforce the fabric on either side of the cut line by working a vertical line of single crochet *(or sewing a line using a sewing machine)* between stitches 2 and 3, and between stitches 3 and 4 of the steek. Next, cut up the middle of stitch 3. Once the cut has been made, you will pick up and work your button bands. To finish, fold over and sew down the small 'flap' created by the steek at the back of the work.

button bands:

Button bands are worked in MC using smaller needles. Pick up and knit stitches each side of the 5 steek sts *(now cut in 1/2)*, that is, before the first stitch of the round, and after the 5th stitch of the round.

Left button band: With RS facing, starting at the top of the left front, pick up and knit approximately 5 sts in every 7 rows, ending with a number that is divisible by 4 plus 2. Make a note of the total sts.

Row 1 (WS): p2, [k2, p2] to end
Row 2 (RS): k2, [p2, k2] to end
Work rows 1-2 a total of 3 (3, 3, 3, 3, 3, 3, **4, 4, 4, 4, 4, 4, 4, 4, 4, 4**) times. Bind off.

Right button band: With RS facing, starting at the bottom right front, pick up and knit the same number of sts as at left button band.

Work rows 1-2 once, then work row 1 once more.

To make a 1 stitch buttonhole: Work to where you want your buttonhole, yo, k2tog.

Buttonhole row (RS): work 5 (5, 7, 7, 7, 7, 7, **9, 9, 9, 9, 9, 11, 11, 13, 13, 13**) buttonholes, evenly spaced

Work rows 1-2 once (**twice**) more for child (**adult**) sizes. Bind off.

finishing:

Using Kitchener stitch, graft the sleeve and body sts at underarms and sew up any remaining underarm gaps. Sew down sides and bottom of pockets. Weave in ends and sew on buttons corresponding to buttonholes.

Wet block the garment once more. If desired, sew ribbon facings to backs of button bands to cover and protect the raw edge of the steek.

CLAYOQUOT TOQUE

geometric Fair Isle  *by Tin Can Knits*

Clayoquot Sound is home to many beasts of feather, fur and fin. Orca whales hunt salmon in the rich and bountiful waters, and put on a show for the tourists. Black bears shamble along the beaches, then head inland to gorge on wildberries. Bald eagles soar overhead, keen eyes searching for their next meal.

sizing: newborn (baby, toddler, child, **adult S, M, L**)
to fit head: 14 (16, 17.5, 19, **20, 21.5, 23**)" around

materials:

Yarn: DK weight yarn in 3 colours
MC: 70 (80, 90, 100, **120, 140, 160**) yds
CC1: 20 (20, 30, 30, **40, 40, 40**) yds
CC2: 10 (10, 15, 15, **20, 20, 20**) yds
*(samples shown in **Sweet Fiber Merino Twist DK** in 'paper birch', 'marshland', 'something blue', and 'sea glass', 'canary', 'spanish coin')*

Needles: US #4 / 3.5mm and US #6 / 4mm *(or as req'd to meet gauge)* 16" circular needle and DPNs in each size

Gauge: 22 sts & 28 rounds / 4" in stockinette on larger needles

Notions: stitch marker, darning needle

14 (16, 17.5, 19, **20, 21.5, 23**)"

Alexa Ludeman ✦ Emily Wessel

chart A: work rounds 1-3

4 st rep

chart B: work rounds
indicated for your size

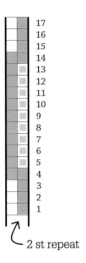

2 st repeat

key & abbreviations:

☐ **MC** - knit with main colour

■ **CC1** - knit with contrast colour 1

▨ **CC2** - knit with contrast colour 2

chart notes:

Charts are read from right to left, all stitches are knit.

When working chart B, refer to pattern instuctions for which rounds to work for your size.

pattern:

Using smaller needles and MC, cast on 72 (80, 88, 92, **100, 108, 116**) sts, PM and join for working in the round. Work in 2x2 ribbing *(k2, p2)* for 0.5 (0.5, 0.75, 0.75, **1.25, 1.25, 1.5**) inches. Switch to larger needles.

Next round: [k18 (20, 22, 11, **12, 13, 14**), m1] to last 0 (0, 0, 4, **4, 4, 4**) sts, knit to end [76 (84, 92, 100, **108, 116, 124**) sts]

Knit 2 rounds in MC.
Work rounds 1-3 from chart A.
Knit 2 rounds in MC.

Newborn and baby sizes: work rounds 2-7 from chart B, then rounds 14-16.
Toddler and child sizes: work rounds 2-9 from chart B, then rounds 14-16.
Adult S and M sizes: work rounds 2-11 from chart B, then rounds 14-16.
Adult L: work rounds 1-17 from chart B.

Knit 2 rounds in MC.
Work rounds 1-3 from chart A.
Knit 2 rounds in MC.

Continuing in MC, knit every round until piece measures 4 (4.5, 4.75, 5, **5.5, 6, 6.25**)" from cast on.

Set up round: [k8 (9, 10, 11, **12, 13, 14**), k2tog, PM, k9 (10, 11, 12, **13, 14, 15**), PM] around [72 (80, 88, 96, **104, 112, 120**) sts]

Round 1: knit
Round 2: [knit to 2 sts before marker, k2tog] around
Work rounds 1-2 a total of 3 (4, 5, 6, **7, 8, 9**) times, until 48 sts remain (6 sts in each section). Then work round 2 four times, until 16 sts remain.

Next round: [k2tog] around   [8 sts]
Break yarn and thread tail through remaining live sts to close top of toque, removing markers.

Weave in all ends. Wet block the toque to even out the colourwork pattern and smooth out crown decreases *(add white vinegar to the soaking water to prevent colours from bleeding)*.

Alexa Ludeman ✦ Emily Wessel

AMMOLITE

a romantic woodsy cowl ✦ *by Alexa Ludeman*

Ammolite is a gemstone found in the Rocky Mountains, a magnificent wilderness that beckons to adventurous souls. Driving through the Rockies is like crossing over into another world, as coastal landscapes change to mountain vistas which in turn give way to the big open skies of the prairies.

sizing: adult short (adult long, wrap around)
finished measurements: 19 (38, 50)" around, 9" tall

materials:

Yarn: 200 (375, 500) yds worsted / aran weight yarn
*(Short and long samples shown in **Sweet Fiber Cashmerino Worsted** in 'pumpkin spice', 'ever grey' and 'olive')*

Needles: US #8 / 5mm 16 (32, 47)" circular needle
(or as req'd to meet gauge)

Gauge: 18 sts & 24 rounds / 4" in stockinette
24 sts & 24 rounds / 4" in ammolite cable

Notions: stitch markers, cable needle, darning needle

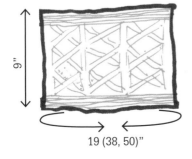

9"

19 (38, 50)"

Alexa Ludeman ✦ Emily Wessel

pattern:

Cast on 80 (160, 218) sts, PM, and join for working in the round.

Work in garter stitch *(knit 1 round, purl 1 round)* until piece measures 1.5 inches, ending with a purl round.

Increase round for adult short and long sizes:
[k1, kfb, k2, kfb] around   [112 (224) sts]

Increase round for wrap around size:
[k1, kfb, k2, kfb] to last 3 sts, k3   [304 sts]

Work rounds 1-12 of ammolite cable a total of three times following chart or written instructions, then work rounds 1-2 once more.

Decrease round for adult short and long sizes:
[p1, p2tog, p2, p2tog] around   [80 (160) sts]

Decrease round for wrap around size:
[p1, p2tog, p2, p2tog] to last 3 sts, p3   [218 sts]

Work in garter stitch for 1.5 inches, starting with a knit round and ending with a purl round. Bind off loosely. Block the cowl and weave in ends. Wear on a romantic walk through the woods!

ammolite cable:

Round 1:   [c4f, p8, c4b] around
Round 2 and all even numbered rounds: work as established, knitting the knits and purling the purls
Round 3:   [k2, t4f, p4, t4b, k2] around
Round 5:   [k2, p2, t4f, t4b, p2, k2] around
Round 7:   [k2, p4, c4b, p4, k2] around
Round 9:   [k2, p2, t4b, t4f, p2, k2] around
Round 11:   [k2, t4b, p4, t4f, k2] around

chart:

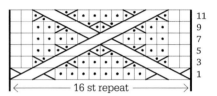

key & abbreviations:

☐ **k** - knit

· **p** - purl

⬲ **c4b** - cable 4 back - slip 2 sts onto cn and hold at back, k2 from LH needle, k2 from cn

⬲ **c4f** - cable 4 front - slip 2 sts onto cn and hold at front, k2 from LH needle, k2 from cn

⬲ **t4b** - twist 4 back - slip 2 sts onto cn and hold at back, k2 from LH needle, p2 from cn

⬲ **t4f** - twist 4 front - slip 2 sts onto cn and hold at front, p2 from LH needle, k2 from cn

chart notes:

Read charts from right to left. Only odd numbered rounds are shown.

All even numbered rounds: knit as established (knit the knits and purl the purls).

CARIBOU

cable yoke cardigan *by Emily Wessel*

The Bow Valley Parkway between Banff and Lake Louise takes you through the heart of the Canadian Rockies. Take time to enjoy the views and you are nearly guaranteed to see wildlife: caribou, elk, bighorn sheep, or perhaps even a grizzly bear.

materials:

Yarn: worsted / aran weight yarn - see table for yardage (*This design requires a blockable yarn. Samples shown in **Brooklyn Tweed Shelter** in 'artifact', 'button jar', 'faded quilt' and 'sap'*)

Needles: US #8 / 5mm and US #6 / 4mm *(or as req'd to meet gauge)* 16-47" circular needle and DPNs in each size

Gauge: 18 sts & 26 rows / 4" in stockinette on larger needles

Notions: stitch markers, cable needle, darning needle, 5 to 13 1/2" to 3/4" buttons

Alexa Ludeman ✦ Emily Wessel

sizing:
sizing: Pattern includes 8 child and 11 adult sizes.

Note: table lists finished garment measurements. Choose a size based on your chest / bust measurement + desired ease.

Size	Chest	Sleeve	Hem to Under-arm	Upper Arm	Yardage
0-3 mo	17"	5.5"	6"	5.5"	300 yds
3-6 mo	18.5"	6.5"	6.5"	7"	350 yds
6-12 mo	20"	7.5"	7.5"	7.5"	400 yds
1-2 yrs	22"	8.5"	8"	8"	450 yds
2-4 yrs	23"	10.5"	10"	8.5"	550 yds
4-6 yrs	24"	12"	12"	9"	600 yds
6-8 yrs	26.5"	13.5"	13"	9.5"	700 yds
8-10 yrs	28"	15"	15"	10.5"	800 yds
XS	**31"**	**17"**	**16"**	**11.5"**	**850 yds**
S	**33"**	**18"**	**16"**	**12"**	**900 yds**
SM	**35"**	**18"**	**17"**	**12.5"**	**1000 yds**
M	**37"**	**19"**	**17"**	**13.5"**	**1100 yds**
ML	**39"**	**19"**	**18"**	**14"**	**1150 yds**
L	**41"**	**20"**	**18"**	**14.5"**	**1250 yds**
LXL	**43"**	**20"**	**19"**	**15"**	**1350 yds**
XL	**47"**	**21"**	**19"**	**16"**	**1500 yds**
XXL	**51"**	**21"**	**20"**	**17"**	**1600 yds**
3XL	**55"**	**21"**	**20"**	**18"**	**1700 yds**
4XL	**59"**	**21"**	**20"**	**19"**	**1800 yds**

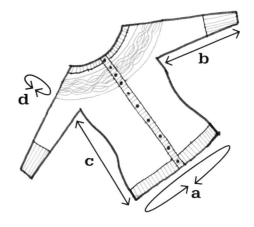

a chest / bust
b sleeve
c hem to underarm
d upper arm

sizing notes: This cardi looks best with 0-2" negative ease for adult sizes, and a bit of positive ease for child sizes. Pattern includes optional waist shaping. Emily (35" bust) is wearing size S with 2" negative ease and waist shaping. Hunter is wearing 2-4 yrs with 1" positive ease. Jones is wearing 1-2 yrs with 2" positive ease. Bodhi is wearing 0-3 mo with 1.5" positive ease.

pattern:

The cabled yoke band is knit first. Stitches are picked up along this band and the neckline is worked to the collar. Next stitches are picked up and the yoke is knit downward. After separation, sleeves and body are knit down to the cuff and hems. Button bands are worked last.

yoke band:

Using larger needles, cast on 22 (**24**) sts for child (**adult**) sizes. *Please note: child size samples shown begin cable on row 13 rather than row 1, and therefore look slightly different than pattern.*

Set up row (WS):
Child sizes: p3, [k1, p2, k1] 4 times, p3
Adult sizes: p4, [k1, p2, k1] 4 times, p4
Work rows 1-4 of chart once, then work rows 1-24 of chart a total of 4 (5, 5, 6, 6, 6, 7, 7, **8, 8, 9, 10, 10, 10, 11, 11, 12, 13, 13**) times, then work rows 1-2 of chart once more. This is a total of 102 (126, 126, 150, 150, 150, 174, 174, **198, 198, 222, 246, 246, 246, 270, 270, 294, 318, 318**) chart rows. Work one more RS row in pattern *(knit the knits, purl the purls)*, then bind off. Wet-block the yoke band in preparation for picking up stitches.

cable panel:

Instructions are for child (**adult**) sizes
*(22 (**24**) stitch panel)*

Rows 1, 3, 7, 9, 11, 13, 15, 19, 21, 23 (RS):
k3 (**4**), [p1, k2, p1] 4 times, k3 (**4**)
Row 2 and all following WS rows:
p3 (**4**), [k1, p2, k1] 4 times, p3 (**4**)
Row 5: k3 (**4**), t8f, t8b , k3 (**4**)
Row 17: k3 (**4**), t8b, t8f, k3 (**4**)

chart: work 22 (**24**) stitch panel for child (**adult**) sizes

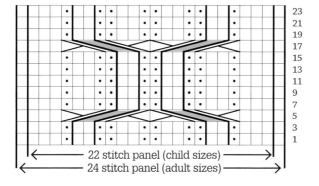

22 stitch panel (child sizes)
24 stitch panel (adult sizes)

chart notes:

Read chart from right to left.

Chart shows RS rows only, all WS rows work in pattern
as established (knit the knits and purl the purls).

key & abbreviations:

☐ **k** - knit

⊡ **p** - purl

t8f - twist 8 front - slip next
4 sts to cn and hold in front
of work, p1, k2, p1 from LH
needle, p1, k2, p1 from cn

t8b - twist 8 back - slip next
4 sts to cn and hold in back
of work, p1, k2, p1 from LH
needle, p1, k2, p1 from cn

Alexa Ludeman ✦ Emily Wessel

upper yoke:

The upper yoke is worked in stockinette stitch, with short row shaping to lift the back neckline.

With larger needles and RS of yoke band facing, pick up and knit 52 (64, 64, 76, 76, 76, 88, 88, **100, 100, 112, 124, 124, 124, 136, 136, 148, 160, 160**) sts along one side of yoke band *(this is approximately 1 stitch in every 2 rows).* Purl 1 row.

Sizes 0-3 mo to 1-2 yrs only: proceed to collar.
Sizes 2-4 and up: work short rows.

Short row 1 (RS): knit to last 14 sts, w&t
Short row 2 (WS): purl to last 14 sts, w&t
Short row 3: knit to 6 sts before wrapped st, w&t
Short row 4: purl to 6 sts before wrapped st, w&t
Repeat short rows 3-4 an additional - (-, -, -, 0, 0, 0, 0, **1, 1, 1, 1, 2, 2, 2, 2, 3, 3, 3**) time(s).

Next 2 rows: Work in pattern to end of row, picking up and working wraps together with wrapped sts.

collar:

Next row (RS): knit, decreasing 0 (9, 0, 9, 6, 0, 9, 0, **6, 3, 15, 27, 24, 24, 33, 33, 42, 54, 54**) sts evenly. [52 (55, 64, 67, 70, 76, 79, 88, **94, 97, 97, 97, 100, 100, 103, 103, 106, 106, 106**) sts]

Switch to smaller needles.

Ribbing (WS): p3, [k1, p2] to last st, p1
Work as established in ribbing for 0.5 (**1**) inches for child (**adult**) sizes. Bind off.

lower yoke:

The lower yoke, body and sleeves are worked in stockinette. With larger needles and RS of yoke band facing, pick up and knit 104, 128, 128, 152, 152, 152, 176, 176, **200, 200, 224, 248, 248, 248, 272, 272, 296, 320, 320**) sts *(approximately 1 st in each row).*

0-3 mo to 1-2 yrs: Purl 1 row.
Sizes 2-4 and up: Work 3 rows in stockinette.

Increase row (RS): knit, increasing 6 (2, 12, 2, 10, 10, 2, 20, **8, 20, 10, 4, 10, 22, 12, 38, 34, 36, 64**) sts evenly [110 (130, 140, 154, 162, 162, 178, 196, **208, 220, 234, 252, 258, 270, 284, 310, 330, 356, 384**) sts]

Work 3 (3, 3, 3, 5, 5, 7, 7, **7, 7, 9, 9, 9, 11, 11, 11, 13, 13, 13**) more rows in stockinette.

separate sleeves and body:

Knit 17 (19, 21, 24, 24, 24, 26, 29, **31, 33, 35, 37, 39, 41, 43, 47, 51, 55, 60**) sts, *(left front)*.

Place next 22 (28, 30, 32, 34, 34, 37, 42, **44, 46, 48, 53, 53, 55, 58, 62, 65, 69, 74**) sts on hold *(left sleeve)*, and cast on 4 (4, 4, 4, 4, 6, 6, 6, **8, 8, 8, 8, 10, 10, 10, 10, 12, 12, 12**) sts using backward loop method *(left underarm)*. *If you plan to work waist shaping, place a marker at the centreline of each underarm section.*

Knit 32 (36, 38, 42, 46, 46, 52, 54, **58, 62, 68, 72, 74, 78, 82, 92, 98, 108, 116**) sts *(back)*.

Place sts on hold for right sleeve as at left, and cast on sts for right underarm as at left. Knit to end of row *(right front)*.

[74 (82, 88, 98, 102, 106, 116, 124, **136, 144, 154, 162, 172, 180, 188, 206, 224, 242, 260**) body sts]

body:

The body is worked in stockinette. Instructions for optional waist shaping for adult sizes given below.

For child sizes, and adult sizes without waist shaping: Work in stockinette until body measures 4.5 (5, 6, 6.5, 8.5, 10.5, 11.5, 13.5, **14, 14, 15, 15, 16, 16, 17, 17, 18, 18, 18**) inches from underarm *(or 1.5 (2) inches short of total desired length for child (adult) sizes)*, ending with a WS row. Proceed to hem.

To incorporate waist shaping (adult sizes): Work in stockinette until body measures **3.25 (3.5, 3.75, 4, 4.25, 4.5, 4.75, 5, 5, 5.25, 5.25)** inches from underarm.

Decrease row (RS): [knit to 4 sts before underarm marker, k2tog, k4, ssk] twice, knit to end   [4 sts dec]
Work 5 rows in stockinette.
Repeat the previous 6 rows three more times. This reduces the stitch count by 16, nipping the waist in 3.5 inches from the bust measurement.

Work 2 more rows in stockinette.

Increase row (RS): [knit to 2 sts before underarm marker, m1, k4, m1] twice, knit to end [4 sts inc]
Work 5 rows in stockinette.

Repeat the previous 6 rows three more times. This increases the total stitch count by 16, back to the total bust dimension. *If desired, you may work further increases at this point to add an inch or two more if your hips are larger than your bust.*

Work in stockinette until body measures **14 (14, 15, 15, 16, 16, 17, 17, 18, 18, 18**) inches from underarm *(or 2 inches short of desired length)*, ending with a WS row. Proceed to hem.

hem:

Decrease for ribbing: knit, decreasing 1 (0, 0, 1, 2, 0, 1, 0, **0, 2, 0, 2, 0, 2, 1, 1, 1, 1, 1**) sts [73 (82, 88, 97, 100, 106, 115, 124, **136, 142, 154, 160, 172, 178, 187, 205, 223, 241, 259**) sts]. *Note: If you used waist shaping and added additional increases at hip, adjust stitch count so it is divisible by a multiple of 3 plus 1.*

Purl 1 row. Switch to smaller needles.

Ribbing (RS): k3, [p1, k2] to last stitch, k1
Work in ribbing as established for 1.5 (**2**) inches for child (**adult**) sizes. Bind off.

sleeves: *(work 2 the same)*

Place 22 (28, 30, 32, 34, 34, 37, 42, **44, 46, 48, 53, 53, 55, 58, 62, 65, 69, 74**) held sts back on larger needles. With RS facing, in underarm stitches, pick up and knit 2 (2, 2, 2, 2, 3, 3, 3, **4, 4, 4, 4, 5, 5, 5, 5, 6, 6, 6**) sts, PM for beginning of round (BOR), pick up and knit 2 (2, 2, 2, 2, 3, 3, 3, **4, 4, 4, 4, 5, 5, 5, 5, 6, 6, 6**) more sts, then knit around held sts and picked-up sts to BOR. [26 (32, 34, 36, 38, 40, 43, 48, **52, 54, 56, 61, 63, 65, 68, 72, 77, 81, 86**) sts]

Knit all rounds until sleeve measures 0.5 (0.5, 0.5, 1, 2, 2, 2, 3, **2, 3, 4, 3, 3, 4, 4, 4, 3, 1, 1**) inches from underarm.

Decrease round: k1, ssk, knit to last 3 sts, k2tog, k1
Knit 5 (5, 5, 5, 5, 5, 5, 5, **5, 5, 5, 5, 5, 4, 4, 4, 4, 4, 3**) rounds.
Repeat previous 6 (6, 6, 6, 6, 6, 6, 6, **6, 6, 6, 6, 6, 5, 5, 5, 5, 5, 4**) rounds an additional 0 (1, 1, 0, 1, 1, 2, 3, **5, 5, 4, 7, 6, 7, 9, 11, 12, 14, 16**) times.
[24 (28, 30, 34, 34, 36, 37, 40, **40, 42, 46, 45, 49, 49, 48, 48, 51, 51, 52**) sts]

Alexa Ludeman ✦ Emily Wessel

Knit all rounds until sleeve measures 3.5, (3.5, 4.5, 4.5, 6.5, 7, 8.5, 10, **11, 12, 12, 13, 13, 13, 13, 14, 14, 14, 14**) inches *(or 2 (3, 3, 4, 4, 5, 5, 5, **6, 6, 6, 6, 6, 7, 7, 7, 7, 7, 7**) inches short of total desired length).*

Next round: knit, decreasing 0 (1, 0, 1, 1, 0, 1, 1, **1, 0, 1, 0, 1, 1, 0, 0, 0, 0, 1**) sts. [24 (27, 30, 33, 33, 36, 36, 39, **39, 42, 45, 45, 48, 48, 48, 48, 51, 51, 51**) sts]

Switch to smaller needles.

Ribbing: k1, [p1, k2] to last 2 sts, p1, k1
Work in ribbing as established until sleeve measures 5.5 (6.5, 7.5, 8.5, 10.5, 12, 13.5 15, **17, 18, 18, 19, 19, 20, 20, 21, 21, 21, 21**) inches, or total desired length. Bind off.

button bands:

Button bands are worked using smaller needles.

Left button band: Start at top of left front, with RS facing. To align the button band ribbing with the cable, you will pick up in three sections; above the cable panel, in the cable panel itself, and below the cable panel. Above the cable panel, pick up and knit approximately 3 sts in every 4 rows, for a total number divisible by 3. Across the cable panel, pick up and knit 2 sts in each stockinette 'rib', and one stitch in each purl 'ditch', for a total of 17 sts in that section. Below the cable panel, pick up and knit approximately 3 sts in every 4 rows, for a total number divisible by 3 in this section. Make a note of the number of sts picked up in each section.

Ribbing (WS): p2, [k1, p2] to end
Work as established in ribbing for 5 (5, 5, 5, 5, 5, 7, 7, **7, 7, 7, 7, 9, 9, 9, 9, 9, 9**) more rows. Bind off.

Right button band: Starting at bottom of right front, with RS facing, pick up and knit the same number of sts in each section as at left button band.

Ribbing (WS): p2, [k1, p2] to end
Work as established in ribbing for 2 (2, 2, 2, 2, 2, 2, 2, **2, 2, 2, 2, 4, 4, 4, 4, 4, 4**) rows.

To make a 1 stitch buttonhole: Work to where you want the buttonhole, yo, k2tog.

Buttonhole row (RS): Work 5-13 buttonholes, evenly spaced in band.

Work 2 (2, 2, 2, 2, 2, 4, 4, **4, 4, 4, 4, 4, 4, 4, 4, 4, 4**) more rows in ribbing, then bind off.

finishing:

Weave in all ends and block your garment. Sew buttons to band opposite buttonholes.

Alexa Ludeman ✦ Emily Wessel

APPLE PIE

a cabled confection  *by Alexa Ludeman*

> Late nights spent driving require frequent stops for sweet sustenance. Check out the local diners, and enjoy some apple pie a la mode!

16 (17.5, 19, 20.5, 22, 23)"

sizing: baby (toddler, child, **adult S, M, L**)
to fit head: 16 (17.5, 19, **20.5, 22, 23**)" around

materials:

Yarn: 90 (130, 150, **200, 220, 240**) yds worsted / aran wt yarn
*(samples shown in **SweetGeorgia Superwash Worsted** in 'saffron', 'deep olive' and 'goldmine')*

Needles: US #6 / 4mm 16" circular needle and US #8 / 5mm
16" circular and DPNs *(or as req'd to meet gauge)*

Gauge: 18 sts & 24 rounds / 4" in stockinette
24 sts & 24 rounds / 4" in apple pie stitch
(gauges given on larger needles)

Notions: stitch marker, cable needle, darning needle, spare
16" circular needle US #6 / 4mm or smaller

Alexa Ludeman ✦ Emily Wessel

pattern:

This hat is knit in the round from brim to crown, and has a doubled over brim.

Using smaller needles, provisionally cast on 72 (76, 80, **88, 92, 96**) sts, PM and join for working in the round.

Work in 2x2 ribbing *(k2, p2)* for 3 (4, 4, **5, 5, 5**) inches. Undo the provisional cast on and place stitches on a spare needle. Fold the ribbing in half, so that the newly added needle, with cast on sts, sits **inside** the needle with the working yarn.

Joining round: With larger needle, [k2tog] around, each time combining one st from the cast on and one st from top of ribbing. [72 (76, 80, **88, 92, 96** sts]

Increase round: [k2, m1, k3, m1] to last 12 (11, 10, **8, 7, 6**) sts, knit to end [96 (102, 108, **120, 126, 132**) sts] Work rounds 1-8 of apple pie stitch pattern until piece measures 4 (5, 6, **7, 8, 8.5**) inches, ending with a round 8 *(for a slouchier hat, work additional repeats at this point).*

Proceed to crown decreases.

apple pie stitch: Repeat rounds 1-8.

Round 1: [p2, k4] around
Round 2: [p2, c4f] around
Round 3: [p2, k4] around
Round 4: [t4b, k2] around
Round 5: k2, [p2, k4] to last 4 sts, p2, k2
Round 6: k2, [p2, c4b] to last 4 sts, p2, then work c4b **over the beginning-of-round marker** as follows: slip 2 sts to cn, hold in back, remove BOR marker, knit 2 sts from LH needle, replace marker, knit 2 sts from cn *(these are the first 2 sts of round 7)*
Round 7: *(note: the first 2 sts of this round have already been worked)* [p2, k4] to last 4 sts, p2, k2
Round 8: [t4f, k2] around

key & abbreviations:

c4f - (cable 4 front) - slip next 2 sts onto cn and hold in front of work, k2 from LH needle, k2 from cn

c4b - (cable 4 back) - slip next 2 sts onto cn and hold in back of work, k2 from LH needle, k2 from cn

t4f - (twist 4 front) - slip next 2 sts onto cn and hold in front of work, p2 from LH needle, k2 from cn

t4b - (twist 4 back) - slip next 2 sts onto cn and hold in back of work, k2 from LH needle, p2 from cn

crown decreases:

Change to DPNs when necessary.

Round 1: [p2tog, k4] around
[80 (85, 90, **100, 105, 110**) sts]

Round 2: [p1, c4f] around

Round 3: [p1, k4] around

Round 4: [p1, k2tog twice] around
[48 (51, 54, **60, 63, 66**) sts]

Round 5: [p1, k2] around

Round 6: [p1, k2tog] around
[32 (34, 36, **40, 42, 44**) sts]

Round 7: [k2tog] around
[16 (17, 18, **20, 21, 22**) sts]

Round 8: [k2tog] to last 0 (1, 0, **0, 1, 0**) sts,
k0 (1, 0, **0, 1, 0**)

[8 (9, 9, **10, 11, 11**) sts]

Cut yarn, leaving an 8 inch tail. Draw the yarn tail through the remaining live sts and pull to close top of hat. Weave in ends and block your hat.

ROMANTIC GETAWAYS

Road tripping is a perfect way to get to know someone. Long hours driving give you a chance to discuss anything and everything as you watch the world go by.

Heading out together with the wind in your hair and adventure ahead is an exciting prospect. You learn a lot about each other, and share the experiences of the road. You hike, picnic, swim, drive late into the night, and find special places that will become your favourite haunts.

When I was sixteen I somehow convinced my parents to let me go on a road trip to a frisbee tournament with my boyfriend. We headed for the Okanagan and talked the whole way. We discussed just about everything under the sun and had a fantastic weekend. It was then that I knew I would marry that man... and seven years later I did!

~ Alexa

RIVULET

textured boho shawl *by Alexa Ludeman*

Summer getaways often lead us to the river, where we may swim, fish or simply relax on the shady riverbank. Hold hands as you follow the path along a mountain stream to find a perfect skinny dipping spot.

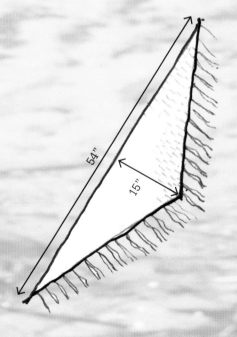

sizing: Finished shawl measures 54" across and 15" deep *(shawl size is easily adjustable but a bigger shawl will change yardage requirements)*

materials:

Yarn: 550 yards sport weight yarn *(sample shown in Plucky Knitter Primo Sport in 'macaroon')*

Needles: US #5 / 3.75mm *(or as req'd to meet gauge)* 32" circular needle

Gauge: 24 sts & 28 rows / 4" in stockinette

Notions: darning needle, crochet hook for fringe

Alexa Ludeman ✦ Emily Wessel

pattern:

This shallow triangular shawl is knit from tip to widest point. Two stitches are increased on each row. Fringe is added last, but to conserve your yarn, you may want to cut it first *(for fringe as shown on page 34, cut 128 ten-inch long pieces, or 256 for double the fringe, as shown in the detail on page 37)*.

Cast on 7 stitches. Purl the first row (WS).

Work rows 1-16 of chart A a total of 7 times, then work rows 1-15 once more. [261 sts]

Note: 32 sts are increased each time chart rows 1-16 are worked. To increase your scarf size, continue in pattern, ending with a chart row 7 or 15.

Bind off all stitches loosely, weave in ends and wet block shawl to size.

fringe:

For each fringe, cut 2 lengths of yarn 10" long. Fold them in half. With WS facing, insert a crochet hook through one of the yarn over holes from WS to RS, pull through a loop of fringe, put fringe ends through the loop and pull tight.

Repeat this process in every other yarn over space for a fringe as shown in sample photo *(on page 34)*, or in every yarn over space for a fuller fringe *(as shown in detail image on page 37)*.

chart notes:

Read RS rows (1, 3, 5, ...) from right to left.

Read WS rows (2, 4, 6, ...) from left to right.

Refer to key for how to work stitches on RS and WS rows.

chart: repeat rows 1-16 seven times, then work rows 1-15 once

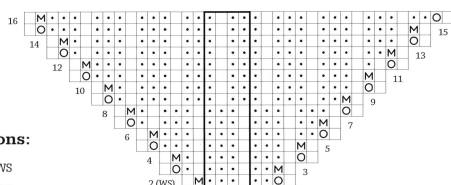

edge sts   4 st repeat   edge sts

key & abbreviations:

☐ **k** - knit on RS, purl on WS

· **p** - purl on RS, knit on WS

○ **yo** - yarn over on RS and WS

M **kfb** - knit front & back on RS and WS

Alexa Ludeman ✦ Emily Wessel

PRAIRIE FIRE

modern lace panel pullover *by Emily Wessel*

Prairie fire grows wild in the alpine at a place called "Meadows in the Sky" near Revelstoke, BC.

Pack a picnic, spread a blanket among the wildflowers, and enjoy a lazy afternoon with good company and exquisite mountain views.

materials:

Yarn: DK / worsted weight yarn - see table for yardage
(*samples shown in* **Madelinetosh Tosh DK** *in 'sequoia' and 'paper'*)

Needles: US #4 / 3.5mm and US #6 / 4mm (*or as req'd to meet gauge*) 16-47" circulars and DPNs in each size

Gauge: 20 sts & 28 rounds / 4" in stockinette on larger needles

Notions: stitch markers, darning needle

Alexa Ludeman ✦ Emily Wessel

sizing: Pattern includes 8 child and 10 adult sizes.

Note: table lists finished garment measurements. Choose a size based upon your chest / bust measurement + desired ease.

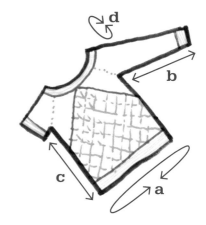

Size	Chest	Long Sleeve	Hem to Under-arm	Upper Arm	Yardage Short / Long Sleeves
0-3 mo	17"	5.5"	6.5"	6"	220 / 200
3-6 mo	18.5"	6"	7"	6.5"	250 / 220
6-12 mo	20.5"	6.5"	8"	7.5"	300 / 250
1-2 yrs	22"	7.5"	8"	7.5"	330 / 300
2-4 yrs	23.5"	9"	9"	8"	450 / 350
4-6 yrs	25"	12"	10"	8.5"	500 / 400
6-8 yrs	27"	13"	13"	9"	650 / 550
8-10 yrs	28.5"	14"	15"	10"	750 / 650
XS	30"	18"	15"	11"	850 / 700
S	33"	18"	16"	12"	950 / 800
SM	34.5"	19"	16"	12"	1050 / 850
M	36"	19"	17"	12.5"	1100 / 950
ML	38"	20"	17"	13.5"	1200 / 1000
L	40"	20"	18"	14.5"	1250 / 1100
XL	44"	21"	19"	16"	1350 / 1150
XXL	48"	21"	19.5"	17"	1450 / 1250
3XL	53"	21"	19.5"	18.5"	1600 / 1400
4XL	59"	21"	22.5"	19.5"	1900 / 1750

a chest / bust
b sleeve
c hem to underarm
d upper arm

sizing notes: Ladies sizes look best with 0-2" negative ease. Child sizes look great with 0-2" positive ease. Lindsay (35" bust) is wearing size SM with 0.5" negative ease, Hunter is wearing 4-6 yrs with 1.5" positive ease. Short sleeves measure 0.5" for 0-3 mo to 1-2 yrs, 1" for 2-4 yrs to adult S, and 1.5" for SM to 4XL.

pattern:

This pullover is knit seamlessly from the collar to hem and cuffs. It can be made with short or long sleeves.

collar:

Using smaller needles, cast on 64 (68, 74, 78, 82, 84, 88, 92, **96, 96, 96, 96, 100, 100, 100, 106, 106, 106**) sts, place marker for BOR and join for working in the round. Purl one round.

Work in garter stitch *(knit 1 round, purl 1 round)* for 6 (6, 6, 6, 8, 8, 8, 10, **10, 10, 10, 12, 12, 12, 12, 14, 14, 14**) rounds. Change to larger needles.

Next round: knit, increasing 2 (2, 12, 8, 12, 14, 14, 10, **14, 18, 22, 26, 22, 26, 30, 36, 52, 80**) sts evenly

[66 (70, 86, 86, 94, 98, 102, 102, **110, 114, 118, 122, 122, 126, 130, 142, 158, 186**) sts]

Alexa Ludeman ✦ Emily Wessel

chart A:

Expanding leaf lace panel.
Work rounds 1-18 once, then repeat rounds
19-24 as many times as noted for your size.

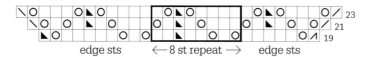

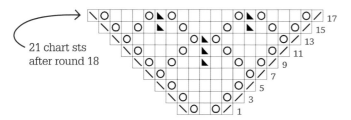

edge sts   ← 8 st repeat →   edge sts

21 chart sts
after round 18

chart B:

Leaf lace pattern in rounds.
Work as many rounds as noted for your size.
Chart B is used for sizes 6-8 years to XXL only.

Before beginning rounds 7, 9,
and 11, remove BOR marker,
knit 1 stitch, replace BOR
marker, then begin chart. This
first stitch is incorporated into
the double decrease at end of
round.

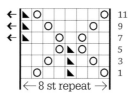

← 8 st repeat →

key & abbreviations:

☐   **k** - knit

◯   **yo** - yarn over

╱   **k2tog** - knit 2 sts together

╲   **ssk** - slip, slip, knit - slip 1
knitwise, slip 1 knitwise,
knit 2 slipped sts together
through back loops

◣   **sl1-k2tog-psso** - slip 1,
k2tog, pass slipped st over

◿   **k3tog** - knit 3 sts together

←   arrow indicates BOR
(beginning of round) shift
at start of round

chart notes:

Charts represent odd numbered rounds only.
Even numbered rounds: knit all sts.
Charts are worked from right to left. Refer to pattern text for
how many repeats to work.

As you can see, the lace panel increases in stitch count each
round, replacing the surrounding stockinette fabric. The
total body stitch count remains the same, but the lace panel
increases by 2 sts each round, except on chart A round 19,
where it increases by 4 sts.

Each chart round is centred over the chart round below. Work
rounds 1-18 of chart A once, then repeat rounds 19-24 as many
times as necessary throughout yoke and body of sweater.

The joining round to join lace from a panel into the round (for
sizes sizes 6-8 years to XXL only) is not shown in charts -
refer to pattern text.

yoke:

To shape the yoke, you increase at 4 raglan increase points. The lace panel begins at centre front, and will continue to increase in width *(the lace replacing the stockinette stitch)* to the hem. The first stitch of the round is the stitch at centre back.

Set up round: knit 12 (13, 15, 16, 17, 18, 19, 19, **19, 21, 22, 23, 23, 23, 25, 27, 30, 36**) sts *(right half of back)*, PM, knit 10 (10, 14, 12, 14, 14, 14, 14, **18, 16, 16, 16, 16, 18, 16, 18, 20, 22**) sts *(right sleeve)*, PM, knit 9 (10, 12, 13, 14, 15, 16, 16, **16, 18, 19, 20, 20, 20, 22, 24, 27, 33**) sts *(right side of front)*, work row 1 of chart A over next 5 sts, knit 9 (10, 12, 13, 14, 15, 16, 16, **16, 18, 19, 20, 20, 20, 22, 24, 27, 33**) sts *(left side of front)*, PM, knit 10 (10, 14, 12, 14, 14, 14, 14, **18, 16, 16, 16, 16, 18, 16, 18, 20, 22**) sts *(left sleeve)*, PM, knit to end *(left half of back)*.

Knit 1 round.

There is a marker at BOR, and 4 raglan markers between back, sleeves, and front, and the location of the lace chart has been established at centre front. From this point forward the lace chart at centre front continues to expand and replace the stockinette stitch either side (refer to chart notes for further details). To shape the yoke, you will increase at the raglan increase points every other round.

Round 1: [knit to 1 st before marker, m1, k2, m1] twice, knit to chart and work next chart round, [knit to 1 st before marker, m1, k2, m1] twice, knit to end   [8 sts inc]
Round 2: knit

Work rounds 1-2 a total of 8 (9, 9, 9, 10, 11, 11, 13, **15, 17, 18, 19, 20, 22, 26, 27, 30, 32**) times. You will have worked a total of 18 (20, 20, 20, 22, 24, 24, 28, **32, 36, 38, 40, 42, 46, 54, 56, 62, 66**) rounds from chart A (this total includes the set up and following knit round).

[130 (142, 158, 158, 174, 186, 190, 206, **230, 250, 262, 274, 282, 302, 338, 358, 398, 442**) sts total; at sleeves: 26 (28, 32, 30, 34, 36, 36, 40, **48, 50, 52, 54, 56, 62, 68, 72, 80, 86**) sts; at front and back: 39 (43, 47, 49, 53, 57, 59, 63, **67, 75, 79, 83, 85, 89, 101, 107, 119, 135**) sts]

Work a further 4 (4, 4, 8, 8, 8, 12, 12, **12, 12, 12, 12, 16, 16, 8, 8, 8, 8**) rounds without increasing at the raglan increase points: simply knit to the chart, work the next chart round, then knit to end.

[total of 22 (24, 24, 28, 30, 32, 36, 40, **44, 48, 50, 52, 58, 62, 62, 64, 70, 74**) rounds worked from chart A to this point]

separate sleeves and body:

At this point you separate the body and sleeves. Continue the lace panel as set at front. Remove all raglan markers.

Knit to first marker, place the next 26 (28, 32, 30, 34, 36, 36, 40, **48, 50, 52, 54, 56, 62, 68, 72, 80, 86**) sts on hold *(right sleeve)*, and cast on 4 (4, 4, 6, 6, 6, 8, 8, **8, 8, 8, 8, 10, 10, 10, 12, 12, 12**) sts *(right underarm)* using the backward loop method.

Work across front, keeping lace panel in pattern, to the next raglan marker. Place sts on hold for left sleeve as at right, cast on for left underarm as at right, then knit to end. Knit 1 round.

The sleeves are now on hold, and there are 86 (94, 102, 110, 118, 126, 134, 142, **150, 166, 174, 182, 190, 198, 222, 238, 262, 294**) body sts on the needle.

The lace panel is 29 (33, 33, 37, 41, 43, 49, 53, **59, 65, 67, 69, 77, 83, 83, 85, 93, 99**) sts wide at this point *(including the decreases either side)*, and there are 57 (61, 69, 73, 77, 83, 85, 89, **91, 101, 107, 113, 113, 115, 139, 153, 169, 195**) stockinette sts remaining.

Work in rounds, continuing lace panel as set and knitting all other stitches. Each time you repeat rounds 19-24, you increase the lace panel by 8 sts, and decrease the stockinette section by 8 sts. Work until there is only one stockinette stitch left *(it should be the first stitch of the round)* and the rest of the stitches are the lace chart *(this will be a further 42 (46, 52, 54, 58, 62, 64, 66, **68, 76, 80, 84, 84, 86, 104, 114, 126, 146**) chart rounds)*. You will end with a chart row 24.

Sizes 0-3 mo to 4-6 yrs, 3XL, 4XL: Stop working lace, and proceed to hem.

Alexa Ludeman ✦ Emily Wessel

Sizes 6-8 yrs to XXL: Work joining round to join the lace panel into a round *(this round not shown on charts)*.

Joining round: remove BOR marker, knit 2 sts *(the knit stitch and the k2tog from the previous chart round)*, replace BOR marker, yo, k5, yo, [k1, yo, k2, sl1-k2tog-psso, k2, yo] repeat to last 9 sts, k1, yo, k5, yo, sl1-k2tog-psso

[2 sts increased; - (-, -, -, -, -, -, 136, 144, **152, 168, 176, 184, 192, 200, 224, 240, -, -**) sts]

Knit 1 round.

To continue lace pattern, work rounds 3-12 of chart B once, then work an additional - (-, -, -, -, -, 6, 18, **18, 18, 12, 12, 12, 18, 6, 0, -, -**) rounds following chart B, starting with round 1.

On rounds 7, 9, and 11 of chart B, there is a double decrease at the end of the round. You must shift the BOR before working these rounds. Remove the BOR marker, knit 1 stitch, replace the BOR marker, then proceed to work the lace pattern as shown on the chart, ending with a sl1-k2tog-psso.

hem:

Switch to smaller needles and work in garter stitch for 0.5 (0.5, 0.5, 0.5, 1, 1, 1, 1, **1, 1, 1.5, 1.5, 1.5, 1.5, 1.5, 1.5, 1.5, 1.5**) inches, or desired length. Bind off.

sleeves: *(work 2 the same)*

Place 26 (28, 32, 30, 34, 36, 36, 40, **48, 50, 52, 54, 56, 62, 68, 72, 80, 86**) held sts back on larger needles. Knit around these sts, then pick up and knit 2 (2, 2, 3, 3, 3, 4, 4, **4, 4, 4, 4, 5, 5, 5, 6, 6, 6**) sts in underarm, place marker for BOR, then pick up and knit 2 (2, 2, 3, 3, 3, 4, 4, **4, 4, 4, 4, 5, 5, 5, 6, 6, 6**) more sts. Knit around to BOR.

[30 (32, 36, 36, 40, 42, 44, 48, **56, 58, 60, 62, 66, 72, 78, 84, 92, 98**) sts]

For short sleeves: Switch to smaller needles and work in garter stitch for 0.5 (0.5, 0.5, 0.5, 1, 1, 1, 1, **1, 1, 1.5, 1.5, 1.5, 1.5, 1.5, 1.5, 1.5, 1.5**) inches, or desired length. Bind off.

For long sleeves: Knit even for 0.5 (1, 0, 2, 3, 6, 7, 8, **9, 8, 7, 7, 7, 7, 6, 9, 7, 6**) inches. *Note: if you plan to add or subtract sleeve length, do it here.*

Decrease round: k1, ssk, knit to last 3 sts, k2tog, k1 Knit 9 (9, 9, 9, 9, 9, 9, 9, **9, 9, 9, 9, 9, 6, 6, 4, 4, 4**) rounds.

Repeat previous 10 (10, 10, 10, 10, 10, 10, 10, **10, 10, 10, 10, 10, 7, 7, 5, 5, 5**) rounds 2 (2, 3, 2, 2, 2, 2, 2, **4, 5, 6, 6, 7, 10, 12, 13, 16, 18**) more times. [24 (26, 28, 30, 34, 36, 38, 42, **46, 46, 46, 48, 50, 50, 52, 56, 58, 60**) sts]

Knit even until sleeve measures 5 (5.5, 6, 7, 8, 11, 12, 13, **17, 17, 18, 18, 19, 19, 20, 20, 20, 20**) inches from underarm (*or 0.5 inches short of desired length for 0-3 mo to 1-2 yr sizes, 1 inch short of desired length for all other sizes*).

Switch to smaller needles, and work in garter stitch for 0.5 inches for 0-3 mo to 1-2 yr sizes, and one inch for all other sizes. Bind off.

finishing:

Weave in all ends and wet-block your sweater, stretching it more or less aggressively to open up the lace pattern and create a more snug or more drapey fit. Since lace is very stretchy, you can adjust the finished size of this garment to some degree through the blocking process.

GRANOLA

crunchy cable and lace socks  *by Alexa Ludeman*

Early mornings after late nights of boozy bonfire reverie call for sticky sweet delights and caffeine. Slip on hand-knit socks, pull a slouchy toque over your camp-bed hair and curl up in a cozy corner of the local bakery.

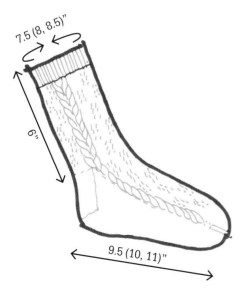

sizing: adult S (M, L)

finished cuff: 7.5 (8, 8.5)" around, 6" long (*adjustable*)

foot length: 9.5 (10, 11)" from heel to toe (*adjustable*)

materials:

Yarn: 320 (340, 360) yds sport weight yarn
(*Sample shown in Madelinetosh Pashmina in 'glazed pecan'*)

Needles: US #2 / 2.75mm and US #3 / 3.25mm DPNs
(*or as req'd to meet gauge*)

Gauge: 28 sts & 36 rounds / 4" in stockinette on larger needles

Notions: stitch markers, darning needle, cable needle

Alexa Ludeman ✦ Emily Wessel

pattern:

These socks are knit in the round from cuff to toe with a standard heel flap, short row heel and gusset construction.

cuff:

With smaller needles cast on 56 (60, 64) sts, PM and join for working in the round.

Ribbing: [k1, p1] around

Work in ribbing as established until piece measures 1.5 inches from cast on. Switch to larger needles and work in pattern following chart or written instructions.

Rounds 1, 3, 5, 7: [k4, p1 (2, 3), k1, [k4, p2, yo, p2tog] twice, k1, p1 (2, 3), k4] twice
Rounds 2 and 6: [k4, p1 (2, 3), k1, [k4, p2tog, yo, p2] twice, k1, p1 (2, 3), k4] twice
Rounds 4 and 8: [c4b, p1 (2, 3), k1, [k4, p2tog, yo, p2] twice, k1, p1 (2, 3), c4f] twice
Rounds 9, 11, 13, 15: [k4, p1 (2, 3), k1, [p2, yo, p2tog, k4] twice, k1, p1 (2, 3), k4] twice
Rounds 10 and 14: [k4, p1 (2, 3), k1, [p2tog, yo, p2, k4] twice, k1, p1 (2, 3), k4] twice
Rounds 12 and 16: [c4b, p1 (2, 3), k1, [p2tog, yo, p2, k4] twice, k1, p1 (2, 3), c4f] twice

Repeat rounds 1-16 until cuff measures 6 inches from cast on (*or desired length*) ending on a round 8 or 16.

chart: repeat rounds 1-16

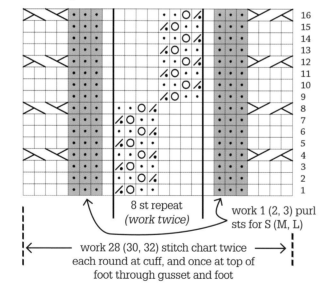

8 st repeat
(work twice)

work 1 (2, 3) purl
sts for S (M, L)

work 28 (30, 32) stitch chart twice
each round at cuff, and once at top of
foot through gusset and foot

key & abbreviations:

☐ k - knit

• p - purl

Ⓞ yo - yarn over

⟋ p2tog - purl 2 together

c4b - cable 4 back - slip 2 sts
to cn, hold at back, k2 from
LH needle, k2 from cn

c4f - cable 4 front - slip 2 sts
to cn, hold at front, k2 from
LH needle, k2 from cn

▨ shade indicates stitches
worked on some sizes, but
not on others

chart notes:

Chart shows all rounds. Read chart from right to left.
Work the number of shaded purl sts as per the directions for your size.

heel flap:

The heel flap is worked over the first 28 (30, 32) sts of the round. You will work back and forth, leaving remaining sts (*top of foot*) on hold.

Row 1: [sl1, k1] 14 (15, 16) times, turn work
Row 2: sl1, p27 (29, 31), turn work

Work rows 1-2 a total of 16 (17, 18) times. There will be 16 (17, 18) slipped sts along each edge of the heel.

heel turn:

Row 1: sl1, k16 (16, 18), ssk, k1, turn work
Row 2: sl1, p7 (5, 7) p2tog, p1, turn work
Row 3: sl1, knit to 1 st before the gap, ssk *(to close the gap)*, k1, turn work
Row 4: sl1, purl to 1 st before the gap, p2tog *(to close the gap)*, p1, turn work

Repeat rows 3-4 until all heel sts have been worked. [18 (18, 20) sts remain at heel]

Knit 9 (9, 10) sts, to centre point of heel sts. This will be the new BOR.

gusset:

Set up round: N1 - knit 9 (9, 10) heel sts, pick up and knit 16 (17, 18) sts along the side of the heel flap.
N2 - work in pattern across the 28 (30, 32) sts at top of foot *(following chart or written instructions)*
N3 - pick up and knit 16 (17, 18) sts along the side of the heel flap, knit to end of round
[78 (82, 88) sts]

Round 1:
N1 - knit to last 3 sts of needle, k2tog, k1,
N2 - work in pattern,
N3 - k1, ssk, knit to end   [2 sts dec]

Round 2: **N1** - knit, **N2** - work in pattern, **N3** - knit

Work rounds 1-2 a total of 11 (11, 12) times. [56 (60, 64) sts]

foot:

Continue working as established (*keeping in pattern across top of foot*) until the foot measures 8 (8.5, 9.5) inches (*or 1.5 inches short of the total desired length*), ending on pattern round 8 or 16.

toe:

Knit to end of N1, this will be the new BOR, located at the side of the foot, at the start of N2.

Round 1: **N2** - k1, ssk, knit to 3 sts before end of needle, k2tog, k1,
N3 - k1, ssk, knit to end of needle,
N1 - knit to last 3 sts, k2tog, k1
[4 sts dec]
Round 2: knit

Work rounds 1-2 a total of 5 (6, 7) times.   [36 sts]
Work round 1 five more times.   [16 sts]

Break yarn, and graft toe closed using Kitchener stitch. Weave in all ends, block your socks to enhance the lace pattern and wear them out to get a latte and a scone!

Alexa Ludeman ✦ Emily Wessel

GRAYLING

delicate cabled mittens  *by Emily Wessel*

Early morning sun rises over the mountains as you unzip the tent and stretch. Time for some eggs and coffee before heading out into the wilderness for a long day of hiking, just you two.

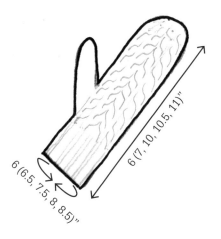

sizing: toddler (child, adult S, M, L)
fits hand: 6 (6.5, 7.5, 8, 8.5)" around at palm
mitten length: 6 (7, 10, 10.5, 11)" cuff to tip

materials:

Yarn: 130 (150, 200, 220, 250) yds sport weight yarn
*(Samples shown in **Madelinetosh Tosh Sport** in 'button jar blue')*

Needles: US #2 / 2.75mm DPNs *(or as req'd to meet gauge)*

Gauge: 26 sts & 38 rounds / 4" in stockinette

Notions: stitch markers, cable needle, darning needle

Alexa Ludeman ✦ Emily Wessel

cable panel A: (toddler & child sizes)

| Round 1: | p1, c3f, p1, c3f, k1, c3b, p1, c3b, p1 |
| Rounds 2, 3, 4: | p1, k3, p1, k7, p1, k3, p1 |

Repeat rounds 1-4.

cable panel B: (adult S, M, L sizes)

| Round 1: | p1 (2, 2), c4f, p1 (2, 2), c4f, k1, c4b, p1 (2, 2), c4b, p1 (2, 2) |
| Rounds 2, 3, 4: | p1 (2, 2), k4, p1 (2, 2), k9, p1 (2, 2), k4, p1 (2, 2) |

Repeat rounds 1-4.

cable panel A:
repeat rounds 1-4 (toddler & child sizes)

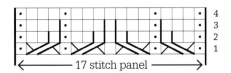

← 17 stitch panel →

cable panel B:
repeat rounds 1-4 (adult S, M, L sizes)

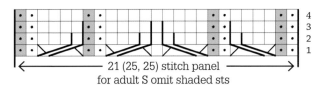

← 21 (25, 25) stitch panel →
for adult S omit shaded sts

key & abbreviations:

☐ **k** - knit

⊡ **p** - purl

c3f - cable 3 front - slip next stitch to cn and hold in front of work, k2 from LH needle, k1 from cn

c3b - cable 3 back - slip next 2 sts to cn and hold in back of work, k1 from LH needle, k2 from cn

c4f - cable 4 front - slip next stitch to cn and hold in front of work, k3 from LH needle, k1 from cn

c4b - cable 4 back - slip next 3 sts to cn and hold in back of work, k1 from LH needle, k3 from cn

▨ shade indicates stitch worked in sizes M and L, but not in size S

chart notes:

Read charts from right to left.
Charts show all rounds.

c3bdec - cable 3 back decrease - slip next 2 sts to cn and hold in back of work, k1 from LH needle, k2tog from cn

c3fdec - cable 3 front decrease - slip next st to cn and hold in front of work, ssk from LH needle, k1 from cn

c4bdec - cable 4 back decrease - slip next 3 sts to cn and hold in back of work, k1 from LH needle, k2tog, k1 from cn

c4fdec - cable 4 front decrease - slip 1 st to cn and hold in front of work, k1, ssk from LH needle, k1 from cn

cuff: Cast on 38 (44, 48, 52, 56) sts, PM and join for working in the round.

Ribbing: Follow instructions for your size.

Toddler, child, S: [p1, k3 (3, 4)] four times, [p1, k1] to end

M and L: [p2, k4] twice, p1, [k4, p2] twice, k1, [p1, k1] to end

Work in ribbing as set for 1 (1, 2.5, 2.5, 2.5) inches.

Next round: Work cable panel A (A, B, B, B) over the first 17 (17, 21, 25, 25) sts, continue in ribbing as established to end of round.

Continue in pattern, working cable panel rounds 1-4 a total of 2 times (8 rounds total). From this point, you will continue the cable pattern as established at back of hand *(continuing to repeat rounds 1-4 throughout mitten)* and work in stockinette at palm.

thumb gusset:

Set up round: For LH mitten: work in pattern across panel, knit to last 4 sts, PM, m1, PM, k4

For RH mitten: work in pattern across panel, k4, PM, m1, PM, knit to end
[1 st inc; 39 (45, 49, 53, 57) sts]

The thumb gusset will be created between the markers, growing from the first newly made stitch.

Round 1: work in pattern across panel, knit to end
Round 2: work in pattern across panel, knit to marker, SM, m1, knit to next marker, m1, SM, knit to end [2 sts inc]
Work rounds 1-2 a total of 7 (7, 8, 9, 10) times, then work round 1 zero (2, 2, 4, 4) more times.
[53 (59, 65, 71, 77) sts total; 15 (15, 17, 19, 21) thumb gusset sts]

Next round: work in pattern across panel, knit to marker, place next 15 (15, 17, 19, 21) sts on hold, removing markers, knit to end
[38 (44, 48, 52, 56) sts]

hand:
Continue in pattern, until piece measures 2 (2.5, 3.5, 3.75, 4) inches from end of thumb gusset *(or 0.75 inches short of total desired length)*, ending with a pattern round 4.

Toddler size: Work round 1 of cable panel A, knit to end [38 sts]

Child size: Work round 1 of cable panel A, k2tog, ssk, ssk, knit to last 6 sts, k2tog, k2tog, ssk [38 sts]

Size S: p1, c4fdec, p1, c4fdec, k1, c4bdec, p1, c4bdec, p1, k2, ssk, k3, ssk, k2, ssk, k1, k2tog, k2, k2tog, k3, k2tog, k2 [38 sts]

Size M: p2tog, c4fdec, p2tog, c4fdec, k1, c4bdec, p2tog, c4bdec, p2tog, k2, [ssk] 3 times, k11, [k2tog] 3 times, k2 [38 sts]

Size L: p2tog, c4fdec, p2tog, c4fdec, k1, c4bdec, p2tog, c4bdec, p2tog, k2, [ssk] 5 times, k7, [k2tog] 5 times, k2 [38 sts]

All sizes: Work rnd 2 of cable panel A, knit to end

Set up round: Remove BOR marker, work round 3 of cable panel A, knit to last stitch, replace BOR marker
Round 1: k1, p1, c3fdec, p1, c3fdec, k1, c3bdec, p1, c3bdec, p1, k2, ssk, k2, ssk, k5, k2tog, k2, k2tog, k1 [30 sts]
Rounds 2 & 4 : knit the knits and purl the purls
Round 3: k1, p1, ssk, p1, k1, sl1-k2tog-psso, k1, p1, k2tog, p1, k2, ssk, k1, ssk, k3, k2tog, k1, k2tog, k1 [22 sts]
Round 5: [k1, ssk, ssk, k1, k2tog, k2tog, k1] twice [14 sts]
Break yarn, leaving a 12 inch tail. Place first 7 sts on one needle, last 7 sts on another, and graft the top of mitten using Kitchener stitch.

thumb:
Place 15 (15, 17, 19, 21) held sts back on needles. Attach yarn, knit these sts, then pick up and knit 3 sts from hand. [18 (18, 20, 22, 24) sts]

Next round: knit to last 3 sts, sl1-k2tog-psso
Knit until thumb measures 1 (1.5, 1.5, 1.75, 2) inches *(or 0.25 inches short of desired length)*.

Round 1:   k1 (1, 0, 2, 1), [k1, k2tog] to end
Round 2:   knit
Round 3:   k1 (1, 0, 0, 1), [k2tog] to end
Break yarn, leaving 6" tail. Draw tail through 6 (6, 6, 7, 8) last sts and pull tight to close thumb.

finishing:
Weave in all ends and block mittens to relax the cable pattern.

VIEWFINDER

a frothy lace cowl *by Alexa Ludeman*

Nestled in the heart of the Rocky Mountains sits a lovely historic hotel on the shores of Lake Louise. Enjoy a little romance and elegance while strolling hand in hand by the iconic glacial waters.

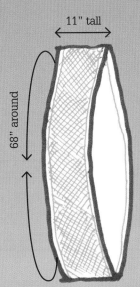

11" tall

68" around

sizing:

Finished cowl measures 68" around and 11" tall after blocking. Finished size varies depending on how aggressively the lace is blocked.

materials:

Yarn: 520 yds lace weight yarn *(sample shown in Indigodragonfly Merino Single Lace in 'don't blink')*

Needles: US #3 / 3.25mm and US #5 / 3.75mm *(or as req'd to meet gauge)* 32" circular needles

Gauge: 16 sts & 36 rounds / 4" over viewfinder lace on larger needles after blocking

Notions: darning needle, stitch marker

Alexa Ludeman ✦ Emily Wessel

pattern:

This cowl is knit in the round.

Using smaller needles cast on 312 sts, PM and join for working in the round being careful not to twist the cast on. Knit 6 rounds. Change to larger needles.

Decrease round: [k4, k2tog] around   [260 sts]

Work Rows 1-4 of viewfinder lace 23 times *(or to desired height, ending with a round 2 or 4, remembering that the piece will grow substantially with blocking).*

Note: lifelines can be very helpful in this pattern. Simply thread a thin piece of yarn or thread, in a contrasting colour, through the live sts. Continue working the project. The lifeline remains in the knitting (don't knit it in) and if a mistake is made you can simply pull out the needles and rip back to the lifeline.

Increase round: [k5, m1] around   [312 sts]

Change to smaller needles. Knit 6 rounds, then bind off loosely.

Weave in ends and wet block your cowl to reveal the lace pattern.

viewfinder lace:

Round 1: [yo, k2tog] around
Round 2 and 4: knit
Round 3: k1, [yo, ssk] to last st, yo, slip 1, remove marker, slip 1 more, knit these two sts together through the back loops, replace marker

Repeat rounds 1-4 for lace pattern.

ROAD TRIP 57

Alexa Ludeman ✦ Emily Wessel

FAMILY MEMORIES

I will always remember the road trips I took with my family when I was young. We would pack up the van with sleeping bags, tents, and a full cooler, and hit the road. No matter which direction we were headed there was the promise of adventure and good times. We never left the Risk board or a deck of cards behind. We were guaranteed to see something new and exciting and enjoy good times around the fire.

Now that I have a few wee kiddos of my own I can see the road trip from the other side. The endless packing and unpacking, the constant state of either making or cleaning up from a meal, and the concerns of toddlers in the vicinity of campfires. But the hard work aside, it is wonderful to see the world through new eyes. When we stop at our favourite spots and our little ones see them for the first time, my enthusiasm is renewed.

~ Alexa

OLD GROWTH

a forest inspired cardigan  *by Alexa Ludeman*

Whether you are little or big, a walk in the woods is a great adventure. Wind your way between ferns and mossy logs, look up to see light filtering down through the forest canopy, and breathe in the vibrant earthiness of this special place.

materials:

Yarn:	worsted / aran weight yarn - see table for yardage *(samples shown in **Plucky Knitter Primo Worsted** in 'naragansette grey' and 'princess phone')*
Needles:	US #8 / 5mm & US #6 / 4mm *(or as req'd to meet gauge)* 32-47" circular needle and DPNs in each size
Gauge:	18 sts & 24 rows / 4" in stockinette on larger needles
Notions:	stitch markers, darning needle, 5 to 11 1/2" to 1" buttons

Alexa Ludeman ✦ Emily Wessel

sizing: pattern includes 7 child and 11 adult sizes.

Note: table lists finished garment measurements. Choose a size based upon your chest / bust measurement + desired ease.

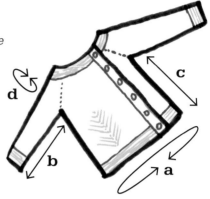

Size	Chest	Sleeve	Hem to Under-arm	Upper Arm	Yardage
0-6 mo	18"	6.5"	7"	6.5"	300 yds
6-12 mo	20"	7.5"	7"	7"	350 yds
1-2 yrs	22"	8.5"	7.5"	7.5"	400 yds
2-4 yrs	24"	10.5"	8"	8"	450 yds
4-6 yrs	26"	12"	10"	8.5"	550 yds
6-8 yrs	28"	13"	13"	9"	700 yds
8-10 yrs	30"	14"	15"	9"	800 yds
XS	32"	16"	15"	10"	900 yds
S	34"	17"	16"	11"	1000 yds
SM	36"	18"	16"	11"	1100 yds
M	38"	19"	17"	11.5"	1200 yds
ML	40"	19"	18"	12"	1300 yds
L	42"	20"	18"	12.5"	1400 yds
LXL	44"	20"	18"	13"	1500 yds
XL	46"	21"	19"	14"	1600 yds
XXL	50"	21"	19"	16"	1800 yds
3XL	54"	21"	20"	17.5"	1900 yds
4XL	58"	21"	20"	19"	2000 yds

a chest / bust
b sleeve
c hem to underarm
d upper arm

sizing notes: This cardi looks best
with -1 to 1" positive ease. Emily (35" bust) is wearing size S (34") with 1" negative ease, Hunter is wearing 4-6 yrs with 2" positive ease.

pattern:

This cardigan is knit seamlessly from the bottom up. Sleeves are worked in the round, and the body in rows to the underarm. Sleeves and body are joined, and the yoke is worked in rows. Button bands are worked last.

sleeves: *(work 2 the same)*

With smaller needles cast on 24 (26, 28, 30, 32, 34, 36, **38, 40, 40, 42, 44, 46, 46, 48, 50, 52, 56**) sts, PM, and join for working in the round.

Work in garter stitch *(knit 1 round, purl 1 round)* until piece measures 2 (2, 2, 2, 2.5, 2.5, 2.5, **2.5, 2.5, 2.5, 3, 3, 3, 3, 3, 3, 3, 3**) inches from cast on. Change to larger needles. Knit 2 rounds.

Increase round: k1, m1, knit to last st, m1, k1
Knit 5 rounds.

Work these 6 rounds a total of 3 (3, 3, 3, 3, 3, 3, **4, 5, 5, 5, 5, 5, 7, 8, 11, 14, 15**) times
[30 (32, 34, 36, 38, 40, 42, **46, 50, 50, 52, 54, 56, 60, 64, 72, 80, 86**) sts]

Knit all rounds until sleeve measures 6.5 (7.5, 8.5, 10.5, 12, 13, 14, **16, 17, 18, 19, 19, 20, 20, 21, 21, 21, 21**) inches from cast on *(or desired length to underarm)*. Knit 2 (2, 2, 2, 3, 3, 3, **3, 3, 4, 4, 4, 4, 4, 5, 5, 5**) sts and place the last 4 (4, 4, 4, 6, 6, 6, **6, 6, 6, 8, 8, 8, 8, 10, 10, 10**) sts on waste yarn *(for underarm)* and remaining sts on a separate piece of waste yarn. *Tip: when breaking yarn leave a 12 inch tail to graft underarm stitches later.*

chart A: Sizes 0-6 mo to 2-4 yr

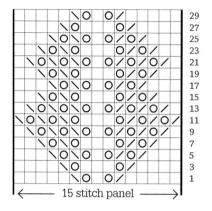

← 15 stitch panel →

chart B: Sizes 4-6 yrs to adult M

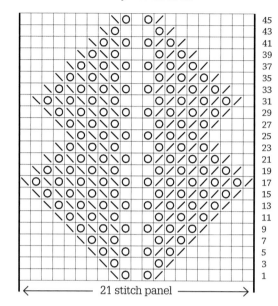

← 21 stitch panel →

key & abbreviations:

☐ **k** - knit

○ **yo** - yarn over

◺ **k2tog** - knit 2 sts together

◹ **ssk** - slip, slip, knit - slip 1 knitwise, slip 1 knitwise, knit 2 slipped sts together through back loops

chart notes:

Read charts from right to left.
Only RS rows are shown in charts.
All WS rows: purl

chart C: Sizes ML to 4XL

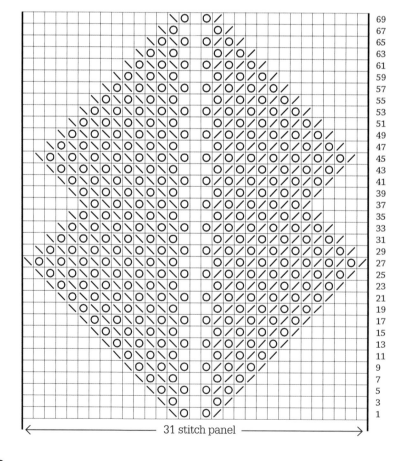

← 31 stitch panel →

body:

Using smaller needles cast on 77 (88, 95, 103, 111, 120, 131, **138, 147, 156, 165, 174, 183, 192, 201, 219, 237, 255**) sts.

Work in garter stitch (*knit every row*) until piece measures 1 (1, 2, 2, 2, 2, 2, **2.5, 2.5, 2.5, 3, 3, 3, 3, 3, 3, 3, 3**) inches, ending with a WS row. Change to larger needles.

Set up row (RS): k6 (7, 8, 10, 10, 10, 11, **12, 14, 16, 18, 14, 16, 17, 20, 23, 26, 30**), PM, k15 (15, 15, 15, 21, 21, 21, **21, 21, 21, 21, 31, 31, 31, 31, 31, 31, 31**), PM, knit to end

Work in stockinette stitch (*knit RS rows, purl WS rows*) for 3 rows.

At this point you will begin working the chart. For sizes 0-6 mo to 2-4 yrs, use chart A, for sizes 4-6 yrs to adult M, use chart B. For sizes ML to 4XL, use chart C.

Row 1 (RS): knit to marker, work chart to marker, knit to end

Row 2 (WS): purl

Repeat rows 1-2 until all charted rows have been worked. Remove markers on final chart row.

Work in stockinette until body measures 7 (7, 7.5, 8, 10, 13, 15, **15, 16, 16, 17, 18, 18, 18, 19, 19, 20, 20**) inches from cast on (*or desired length to underarm*), ending with a WS row.

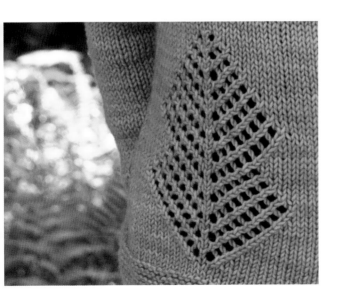

join sleeves and body for yoke:

Knit 22 (27, 30, 31, 33, 37, 40, **42, 44, 47, 49, 52, 56, 58, 63, 68, 75, 81**) sts (*right front*), place next 4 (4, 4, 4, 6, 6, 6, **6, 6, 6, 8, 8, 8, 8, 8, 10, 10, 10**) sts on hold (*right underarm*), PM.

Knit 26 (28, 30, 32, 32, 34, 36, **40, 44, 44, 44, 46, 48, 52, 56, 62, 70, 76**) held sts from right sleeve (*all except the underarm sts*), PM.

Knit 36 (41, 44, 50, 52, 55, 60, **64, 69, 74, 76, 81, 85, 90, 94, 101, 110, 119**) sts (*back*). Place sts on hold for left underarm as at right, PM.

Knit held sts from left sleeve as at right, PM.

Knit 11 (12, 13, 14, 14, 16, 19, **20, 22, 23, 24, 25, 26, 28, 28, 30, 32, 35**) remaining sts (*left front*).

[121 (136, 147, 159, 163, 176, 191, **206, 223, 232, 237, 250, 263, 280, 297, 323, 357, 387**) sts]

Work 5 (3, 3, 3, 5, 5, 7, **5, 3, 3, 3, 3, 3, 3, 3, 3, 3**) rows in stockinette.

yoke:

Row 1 (RS): [knit to 3 sts before marker, ssk, k2, k2tog] 4 times, knit to end   [8 sts dec]

Row 2 (WS): purl

Work rows 1-2 a total of 7 (8, 9, 10, 10, 12, 13, **14, 16, 17, 18, 19, 20, 22, 22, 24, 26, 29**) times.

[65 (72, 75, 79, 83, 80, 87, **94, 95, 96, 93, 98, 103, 104, 121, 131, 149, 155**) sts]

Next row: knit, decreasing 9 (10, 7, 5, 9, 4, 9, **8, 9, 8, 5, 8, 13, 12, 29, 37, 53, 59**) sts evenly

[56 (62, 68, 74, 74, 76, 78, **86, 86, 88, 88, 90, 90, 92, 92, 94, 96, 96**) sts]

Remove all markers, switch to smaller needles and work in garter stitch for 1 (1, 2, 2, 2, 2, 2, **2.5, 2.5, 2.5, 2.5, 2.5, 2.5, 2.5, 2.5, 2.5, 2.5, 2.5**) inches. Bind off.

Alexa Ludeman ✦ Emily Wessel

button bands:

Button bands are worked using smaller needles.

Left button band: With RS facing, starting at the top of left front, pick up and knit approximately 3 sts in every 4 rows. Take note of total sts picked up. Knit 6 (6, 10, 10, 10, 10, 10, **14, 14, 14, 14, 14, 14, 14, 14, 14, 14, 14**) rows. Bind off.

Right button band: With RS facing, starting at the bottom of right front, pick up and knit the same number of sts as for left button band. Knit 3 (3, 5, 5, 5, 5, 5, **7, 7, 7, 7, 7, 7, 7, 7, 7, 7**) rows.

To make a 2-st buttonhole in 1 row: Slip next 2 sts pass the first st over the second (*one st bound off*), sl1, bind stitch off. Slip stitch from RH needle to LH needle. Using backward loop method, cast on 2 sts. Proceed to next buttonhole.

Note: If you find this buttonhole is too big or too small, you can work similar buttonholes by binding off then casting on 1 or 3 sts in the same manner.

Buttonhole row (RS): Work 5 to 11 buttonholes evenly spaced in band.

Knit 2 (2, 4, 4, 4, 4, 4, **6, 6, 6, 6, 6, 6, 6, 6, 6, 6**) more rows. Bind off.

finishing:

Using Kitchener stitch, graft the sleeve and body sts at underarms and sew up any remaining gaps. Block the cardigan, weave in ends, and sew on buttons corresponding to buttonholes. Wear your new sweater on a walk through the woods!

Alexa Ludeman ✦ Emily Wessel

STOVETOP

a slouchy cabled classic  *by Alexa Ludeman*

The beach is a magnificent place to spend a day with the family. You can walk barefoot along the sand, run from the waves, and dare each other to go into the cold ocean for a swim.

sizing: baby (toddler, child, **adult S, M, L**)
fits head: 16 (18, 20, **21, 22, 23**)" around
finished length: 7.5 (9.25, 10.5, **10.5, 10.5, 11**)"

materials:

Yarn: 90 (120, 140, **170, 185, 200**) yds worsted / aran wt yarn
*(samples shown in **Sweet Fiber Merino Twist Worsted** in 'moss', 'paper birch', and 'charcoal', sizes child, adult M, L)*

Needles: US #6 / 4.0mm 16" circular
US #8 / 5.0mm 16" circular and DPNs
(or as req'd to meet gauge)

Gauge: 18 sts & 24 rounds / 4" in stockinette on larger needles

Notions: cable needle, stitch markers, darning needle

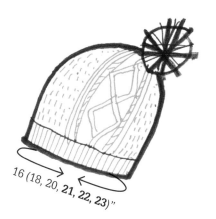

16 (18, 20, **21, 22, 23**)"

Alexa Ludeman ✦ Emily Wessel

pattern:

Using smaller needles cast on 72 (76, 80, **84, 88, 96**) sts, PM, and join for working in the round. Work in 2x2 ribbing *(k2, p2)* until piece measures 0.5 (1, 1, **1.5, 1.5, 2**) inches from cast on.

Set up round: Switch to larger needles.

Baby (toddler, -, -, adult M, L): p25 (25, -, -, **35, 35**), PM, purl to end increasing 1 (3, -, -, **3, 3**) sts evenly

Child (adult S): p25 (**35**), PM, p2tog, purl to end

[73 (79, 79, **83, 91, 99**) sts]

cable pattern:

Follow chart A for baby, toddler and child sizes and chart B for adult sizes. Work 25 (**35**) stitch panel to marker, then work moss stitch to end of round. Only odd numbered rounds are shown in charts; even numbered rounds, work as established (knit the knits and purl the purls).

Baby and child sizes: work rounds 1-16 of chart A 2 (-, **3**) times, then work rounds 1 and 2 once more.

Toddler: work rounds 9-16 of chart A once, work rounds 1-16 twice, then work rounds 1 and 2 once more.

Adult S (M, L): work rounds 1-20 of chart B twice, then work rounds 1 and 2 once more.

decreases: *switch to DPNs as req'd.*

Baby (toddler, child):

Round 1: k1, p1, k4, [p2tog] twice, k1, k2tog, k2, [p2tog] twice, k4, p1, k1, [(k1, p1) twice, k2tog] to end [60 (65, 65) sts]

Rounds 2, 4, and 6: Work as established

Round 3: k1, p1, [c4b, p2] twice, c4f, p1, k1, [p1, k1, p1, k2tog] to end [52 (56, 56) sts]

Round 5: k1, p1, [k2tog, k2tog, p2tog] twice, [k2tog] twice, p1, k1, [k1, p1, k2tog] to end [36 (39, 39) sts]

Round 7: k1, [p1, k2tog] 3 times, p1, k1, [p1, k2tog] to end [25 (27, 27) sts]

Round 8: [k2tog] 4 times, k1, [k2tog] to end [13 (14, 14) sts]

Adult S (M, L):

Round 1: k1, p2tog, k6, [p2tog] twice, p2, k2, k2tog, k1, p2, [p2tog] twice, k6, p2tog, k1, [(k1, p1) 3 times, k2tog] to end [70 (77, 84) sts]

Round 2, 4, 6, 8, and 10: Work as established

Round 3: k1, p1, c6b, [p2tog] twice, c4b, [p2tog] twice, c6f, p1, k1, [(p1, k1) twice, p1, k2tog] to end [60 (66, 72) sts]

Round 5: k1, p1, k2tog, k2, k2tog, p2tog, k4, p2tog, k2tog, k2, k2tog, p1, k1, [(k1, p1) twice, k2tog] to end [48 (53, 58) sts]

Round 7: k1, p1, c4b, p1, c4b, p1, c4f, p1, k1, [p1, k1, p1, k2tog] to end [42 (46, 50) sts]

Round 9: k1, [p1, k2tog, k2tog] 3 times, p1, k1, [k1, p1, k2tog] to end [30 (33, 36) sts]

Round 11: k1, [p1, k2tog] 3 times, p1, k1, [p1, k2tog] to end [21 (23, 25) sts]

Round 12: [k2tog] 4 times, k1, [k2tog] to end [11 (12, 13) sts]

finishing: Cut yarn, leaving a 6 inch tail. Draw tail through remaining sts and secure. Weave in ends and wet-block hat. Make and sew on a pompom if desired.

chart A: for baby, toddler, and child sizes

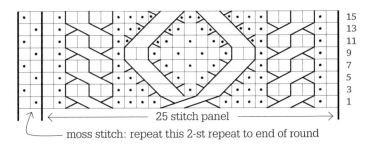

← 25 stitch panel →

↑ — moss stitch: repeat this 2-st repeat to end of round

chart B: for adult S, M, L sizes

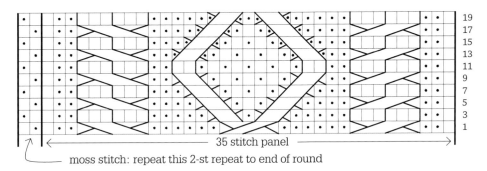

← 35 stitch panel →

↑ — moss stitch: repeat this 2-st repeat to end of round

chart notes:

Charts are read from right to left.

Charts show odd numbered rounds only.

Even numbered rounds: work as established: knit the knits and purl the purls.

key & abbreviations:

☐ **k** - knit

⬚ **p** - purl

c3f (cable 3 front) - slip next 2 sts onto cn and hold in front of work, k1 from LH needle, k2 from cn

c3b (cable 3 back) - slip next st onto cn and hold in back of work, k2 from LH needle, k1 from cn

t3f (twist 3 front) - slip next 2 sts onto cn and hold in front of work, p1 from LH needle, k2 from cn

t3b (twist 3 back) - slip next st onto cn and hold in back of work, k2 from LH needle, p1 from cn

c4f (cable 4 front) - slip next 2 sts onto cn and hold in front of work, k2 from LH needle, k2 from cn

c4b (cable 4 back) - slip 2 sts onto cn and hold in back of work, k2 from LH needle, k2 from cn

c5b (cable 5 back) - slip next 3 sts onto cn and hold in back of work, k2 from LH needle, k3 from cn

c6f (cable 6 front) - slip next 3 sts onto cn and hold in front of work, k3 from LH needle, k3 from cn

c6b (cable 6 back) - slip 3 sts onto cn and hold in back of work, k3 from LH needle, k3 from cn

ROAD TRIP   71

Alexa Ludeman ✦ Emily Wessel

PADDLE

simply stripey mitts *by Alexa Ludeman*

Whether you are paddling your canoe across Moraine Lake or sipping a spiked coffee at the campsite, these simple stripey mitts will keep your hands toasty and your fingers free.

sizing: toddler (child, adult S, M, L)
fits hand: 6 (6.5, 7, 7.75, 8.5)" around at palm
mitten length: 5.5 (6.75, 8.5, 9.25, 10.5)" cuff to tip

materials:

Yarn: DK weight yarn in 2 colours
MC: 50 (70, 100, 120, 140) yds
CC: 15 (20, 25, 30, 40) yds
*(samples shown in **Madelinetosh Tosh DK** in 'silver fox', 'tart', 'cousteau', 'chamomile', and jade')*

Needles: US #3 / 3.25mm and US #5 / 3.75mm DPNs
(or as req'd to meet gauge)

Gauge: 24 sts & 28 rounds / 4" in stockinette on larger needles

Notions: stitch markers, darning needle

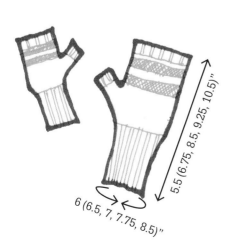

5.5 (6.75, 8.5, 9.25, 10.5)"

6 (6.5, 7, 7.75, 8.5)"

Alexa Ludeman ✦ Emily Wessel

pattern:

These fingerless mitts are knit in the round from cuff to tip. The thumb is worked last. Make 2 the same.

With smaller needles and MC cast on 32 (36, 40, 44, 48) sts, PM and join for working in the round.

Work in 2x2 ribbing *(k2, p2)* until cuff measures 1 (1.5, 2.5, 2.5, 2.5) inches from cast on.

Switch to larger needles and continue working in ribbing as established until piece measures 2 (2.5, 3, 3.5, 4) inches from cast on. Knit 3 rounds.

thumb gusset:

Round 1: m1, k2, m1, PM, knit to end [2 sts inc] The thumb gusset increases between the BOR marker and this second marker.

Round 2: knit

Round 3: m1, knit to marker, m1, SM, knit to end [2 sts inc]

Round 4: knit

Work rounds 3-4 a total of 3 (3, 5, 5, 6) times. There will be 10 (10, 14, 14, 16) sts between the markers.

Knit 0 (2, 4, 4, 6) more rounds.

Next round: Place the first 10 (10, 14, 14, 16) sts on waste yarn, cast on 2 sts using backward loop method, knit to end. [32 (36, 40, 44, 48) sts]

hand:

Knit 1 round in MC. Knit 3 (3, 4, 4, 4) rounds in CC. Knit 2 rounds in MC. Knit 3 (3, 4, 4, 4) rounds in CC. Knit 1 round in MC.

Change to smaller needles and work in 2x2 ribbing for 0.5 (0.75, 1, 1.25, 1.5) inches. Bind off loosely.

thumb:

Place 10 (10, 14, 14, 16) held thumb sts onto larger needles. Knit across these sts, pick up 2 sts from hand, PM, and join for working in the round. [12 (12, 16, 16, 18) sts]

Knit 2 (2, 3, 3, 3) rounds.

Adult L only: ssk, knit to last 4 sts, k2tog, k2 [- (-, -, -, 16) sts]

All sizes: Change to smaller needles and work in 2x2 ribbing for 0.5 (0.5, 0.75, 0.75, 0.75) inches.

Bind off loosely. Weave in ends, block your mitts, and wear them while paddling the blue lakes of the Rocky Mountains!

ROAD TRIP 75

Alexa Ludeman ✦ Emily Wessel

BONFIRE

wrapped in cables  by Alexa Ludeman

After a long day of tide pool treasure hunting, sandy kids curl up next to the beach bonfire. Parents enjoy a moment of peace and stay up late to share a bottle of wine and laughter around the fire. Snuggled under a warm blanket you can spend a night counting stars.

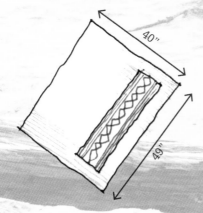

sizing: Finished blanket measures 40" wide by 49" long

materials:

Yarn: 900 yds super bulky weight yarn *(sample shown in Cascade Lana Grande in 'silver grey')*

Needles: US #15 / 10mm 40" circular needle *(or as req'd to meet gauge)*

Gauge: 8 sts & 18 rows / 4" in garter stitch panel repeat measures 13.5" wide by 5.5" high

Notions: stitch markers, cable needle, darning needle

Alexa Ludeman ✦ Emily Wessel

pattern:

Cast on 84 sts. Knit each row until piece measures 3.5 inches from cast on.

Next row (RS): k8, PM, m1, k11, m1, k10, m1, k10, m1, PM, knit to end [88 sts]

There are 35 sts between the markers, this is where the cable panel will be worked. All other stitches will be worked in garter stitch (*knit on all rows*).

Set up row (WS): knit to marker, p1, k2, p6, k6, p5, k6, p6, k2, p1, knit to end

Begin cable panel:

RS rows: knit to marker, work chart to marker, knit to end

WS rows: knit to marker, work in pattern as established (knit the knits and purl the purls) to marker, knit to end

Continue as established, working chart rows 1-20 a total of 8 times (*or to 3.5 inches short of desired length, ending with chart row 20*), then work row 1 once more.

Next row (WS): *(remove markers)* knit to marker, k2tog, [k9, k2tog] three times, knit to end [84 sts]

Knit each row until garter edge measures 3.5 inches. Bind off, weave in ends, and block your blanket. Snuggle up on the beach with someone cute!

chart: repeat rows 1-20

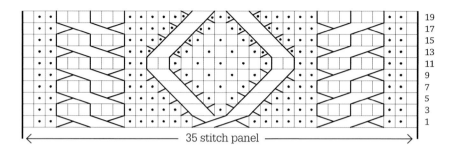

19
17
15
13
11
9
7
5
3
1

← 35 stitch panel →

chart notes:

Charts are read from right to left.
Charts show RS rows only.
WS rows: work as established (knit
the knits and purl the purls)

key & abbreviations:

☐ **k** - knit

· **p** - purl

c3f (cable 3 front) - slip next 2 sts onto
cn and hold in front of work, k1 from
LH needle, k2 from cn

c3b (cable 3 back) - slip next st onto
cn and hold in back of work, k2 from
LH needle, k1 from cn

t3f (twist 3 front) - slip next 2 sts onto
cn and hold in front of work, p1 from
LH needle, k2 from cn

t3b (twist 3 back) - slip next st onto cn
and hold in back of work, k2 from LH
needle, p1 from cn

c5b (cable 5 back) - slip next 3 sts onto
cn and hold in back of work, k2 from
LH needle, k3 from cn

c6f (cable 6 front) - slip next 3 sts onto
cn and hold in front of work, k3 from
LH needle, k3 from cn

c6b (cable 6 back) - slip 3 sts onto cn
and hold in back of work, k3 from LH
needle, k3 from cn

Alexa Ludeman ✦ Emily Wessel

Techniques

This book is intended as a pattern collection, not a reference book. For more in-depth discussion of these and other techniques, visit www.tincanknits.com.

blocking: Blocking is the final piece in any knitting puzzle. **Do not skip this important step!** Blocking consists of washing your knit and letting it dry so the stitches relax into their final form. Blocking radically improves most knitted projects by evening out the stitches. For Fair Isle and lace projects blocking is crucial. To block lace, allow it to soak until fully saturated, squeeze out as much water as possible in a towel, then pull it tightly and pin it into place. Leave the piece until completely dry, then unpin and 'voila' the lace pattern is revealed.

cables & twisted stitches: Cables and twisted stitches are methods of knitting stitches out of regular order to create twists in the fabric. To work cables, you use a cable needle to put a number of stitches on hold, while you knit stitches further along the row. Then you knit the earlier stitches, and the swap creates a twist in the fabric itself. Brilliant and dead easy - try it!

charts: Each chart square represents a stitch as indicated by the key. Repeats are indicated by heavy lines, and are worked as many times as will fit in each round or row. As you will notice, some charts illustrate every row (or round), and others illustrate only RS or odd numbered rows (or rounds), with the WS or even numbered rows or rounds described by text instructions. Always refer to chart notes and key before you begin.

Fair Isle / stranded knitting: Stranded knitting uses two or more colours of yarn at a time to create multicoloured patterns. You knit a number of sts with one colour, then switch to the other colour, and knit a few more. The yarn not currently in use is carried loosely behind the work, creating 'floats'. It is important to relax and allow these floats to be very loose, so the fabric maintains elasticity and does not pull in too much. Another consideration when working stranded patterns is 'yarn dominance'. Essentially, the yarn that is brought up from underneath the other is more dominant and creates slightly larger and more 'dominant' stitches. When working a pattern, consider which colour you want to 'pop' more, and carry that yarn on the bottom consistently.

gauge: Gauge is a measurement of the size of the knit stitches. To knit a sweater that comes out the size you expect, you must begin by making a gauge swatch. Cast on 6 inches worth of stitches, and work in stockinette until you have a 6 inch square. Wet-block the swatch and allow it to dry flat. Then measure the number of stitches and rows in a 4 inch square of fabric. If the gauge you have achieved in the swatch is more stitches than desired, the stitches are too small, so try again on larger needles. If the gauge it is less stitches than desired, the stitches are too big so try again on smaller needles, until you have achieved the pattern gauge.

increase / decrease stitches evenly: OK, so you have seen this instruction, and you probably hate us now. But we would like to humbly suggest you untwist your skivvies and learn a skill or two.

Take it slowly. You have 150 sts on the needles. You are meant to increase 20 sts evenly. 150 / 20 is 7.5. So simply increase 1 stitch after 7 sts [k7, m1] a total of 20 times, then knit whatever sts remain without increasing.

OR the converse (a little more complicated...) You have 150 sts, and are instructed to dec 20 sts evenly. 150 / 20 = 7.5. So 7 is the largest whole number that goes into 150. So you can work [k5, k2tog] (that's 7 stitches) 20 times, then knit the remaining stitches to end of round.

If you have 150 sts, and you're told to decrease 7, evenly spaced, well, essentially... who cares where you put them. [Knit a bunch, k2tog] seven times. It's EASY. What's the bottom line here, ladies and gentlemen? Repeat it with me now... It's EASY!

kitchener stitch: Kitchener stitch, also known as 'grafting' or 'weaving' is a seamless method to join stitches. It essentially forms a new row in between two rows of live stitches. With a darning needle and yarn weave back and forth across the gap, maintaining the looping pattern of the knitted fabric.

pick up and knit stitches: With RS facing, insert needle between sts (or rows), yarn over with working yarn on WS, and pull a loop through knitted fabric to RS (*one st picked up and knit*). Repeat until desired sts have been picked up and knit.

Alexa Ludeman ✦ Emily Wessel

provisional cast on (crochet chain method):

Using waste yarn, crochet a chain a few sts longer than you plan
to cast on. With knitting needles and working yarn, insert needle
under back bump of last crochet chain stitch. Yarn over and pull
up a stitch. Continue along crochet chain, creating as many sts as
required. To 'unpick' the provisional cast on, unfasten the end of the
crochet chain and it will 'unzip', leaving live sts ready to be worked.

put stitches on hold:
Instead of binding off, thread a piece
of waste yarn through the live stitches, so they don't unravel, and then
remove the needles. You may alternately choose to use a stitch holder,
but we generally suggest using waste yarn, as it is pliable and does
not pull on the stitches.

short row shaping:
To work short rows, you knit part
of the way through a row, then stop and turn around before the
end. Work as pattern specifies to the point where it says 'w&t' or
'wrap and turn'. This involves wrapping the working yarn around
the next (unworked) stitch; bring yarn to front, slip next stitch from
LH to RH needle, bring yarn to back, slip stitch back from RH to LH
needle, then turn work. Proceed to work back in opposite direction.
When the pattern says 'pick up wraps' this means you will work the
wrap together (k2tog or p2tog) with the stitch it is wrapped around.

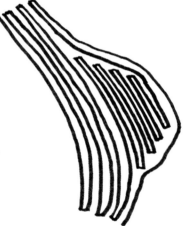

yarn substitutions:
So much love and time goes into
your knits, so spend the money on quality materials for best
results. We recommend wool because is very forgiving (stretchy),
can be blocked to adjust size, and makes for beautiful projects.
For easy care we suggest machine-washable wools. Sock yarns
are particularly well-suited to projects intended for babies; if held
double a sock yarn can substitute for a worsted / aran weight yarn.
Keep in mind that if you are making an adjustment to the pattern
(adding length, width, pattern repeats etc.) this will change your
yardage requirements!

ABBREV.

BOR	beginning of round (marker)
c4b	cable 4 back - for all cable definitions, refer to key and abbreviations in each pattern
CC	contrast colour
cn	cable needle
dec	decrease(d)
DPNs	double pointed needles
inc	increas(ed)
k	knit
k2tog	knit 2 stitches together
k3tog	knit 3 stitches together
kfb	knit into the front and back of one stitch
k-tbl	knit through the back loop of stitch
LH	left hand
m1	make one knit stitch (any method)
m1p	make one purl stitch (using LH needle, lift bar between sts, and purl through front loop
MC	main colour
N1 (2, 3)	needle 1 (2, 3) of DPNs
p	purl
p2tog	purl 2 stitches together
p3tog	purl 3 stitches together
PM	place maker

rep	repeat
req'd	required
RH	right hand
RS	right side of the work (public side)
sl1	slip one stitch (purlwise unless stated otherwise)
sl1-k2tog-psso	slip 1 knitwise, knit 2 together, pass slipped stitch over
SM	slip marker
ssk	slip 2 stitches knitwise (one at a time), then knit 2 slipped stitches together through back loops
st(s)	stitch(es)
t4f	twist 4 front - for all twist definitions, refer to key and abbreviations in each pattern
tbl	through back loop(s) of stitch(es)
w&t	short row wrap & turn
work as established or 'as set' or 'in pattern'	continue in pattern; knit the knit stitches and purl the purls from the previous row. In lace, you typically knit the yo sts (or purl on the WS) and purl the p2togs (or knit on the WS)
WS	wrong side of the work (private side)
yds	yards
yo	yarn over (yarn forward / yfwd)

KNITS YOU WILL LOVE

creating beloved hand knits:

There are many ways to skin a cat, and many methods for wrapping your beloved babes in hand-knits! If you are intending to face the sweater curse head-on, I wish you the best of luck and hope you will consider the following tips and suggestions.

An ill-fitting sweater is probably not cause for a dumping... But let's not take the chance! The best way to knit a sweater that will work for the wearer is to base it upon one that you, he, or she already likes. Lay the sweater flat on the floor and measure:

1. Chest / bust
2. Sleeve length from underarm to cuff
3. Body length from underarm to hem

Armed with these critical dimensions, you can choose the correct size from the pattern options, and determine how to adjust arm and body lengths (if at all). For most situations, this is all that you will need to change.

I don't care if you knit a gauge swatch... because I don't care if your sweater fits. But you should! Many knitters have met desperate and depressing ends due to the TERRIBLE decision to skip the swatch. I hope it won't happen to you...

seamless sweaters:

The garments in this collection are virtually seamless, knit either from the bottom up, or from the top down. Sleeves are knit in the round, and the body is knit in the round or in rows. The yoke of the garments are knit all at once. We design our patterns this way because it is simple, non-fussy, and that is how we like to knit them!

FAV sweater

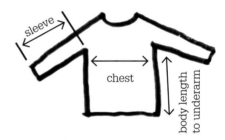

seamless sweater

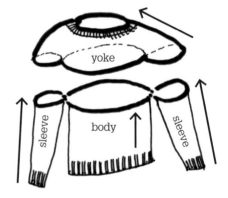

A seamless sweater is a series of tubes:

3 tubes (sleeve, body, sleeve) join to become one BIG tube (yoke) which decreases to a little head-sized tube at the collar. Like magic - it's a sweater!

simple adjustments for a perfect fit:

gorilla arms? Standard sleeve and body lengths are given in our patterns, but for a perfectly customized knit, these are very simple places to adjust - simply knit longer (or shorter) in the body or in the arms.

shorter sleeves? A couple of the designs in this book would look cute with 3/4 length or elbow-length sleeves. This is simple to achieve. Take a look at the number of stitches at the cuff, and the number of stitches at the upper arm, and cast on or decrease to a number somewhere in between.

curvilicious? Some of our patterns do not include waist shaping, because this keeps them simple and unisex. We think they look pretty fabulous without shaping, but you may choose to add it in. The goal is to pinch the stitch count in at the waist, so decrease gradually leading up to the waist point, and then increase gradually again after the waist.

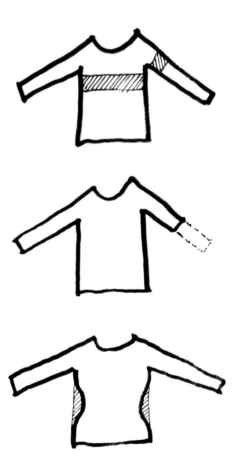

Alexa Ludeman ✦ Emily Wessel

THE CREW

I photographed 'Road Trip' this summer on two real family road trips: one to Tofino on the west coast of Vancouver Island, and the other to Banff in the Rocky Mountains. On the first trip I was pregnant and on the second, 6 weeks later, we took our 3-week-old baby girl on her first camping trip!

Travelling to Tofino involves a ferry ride and a beautiful drive through the mountains. Everybody was very patient, and put up with what seemed like hundreds of lens and wardrobe changes. Between shoots we enjoyed nature walks, fun on the beach, and delicious eats at Big Daddy's Fish Fry.

For Banff we packed the whole family and a LOT of camping supplies into the Jeep. We all love a good camping trip and we were excited to introduce Bodhi to the Canadian wilderness. She seemed to love the fresh air of the Rocky Mountains, and was unfazed by the lack of baths and the cold nights. It was all hands on deck with three kids and Emmy and Juju fulfilled their auntie and uncle duties with gusto. We saw wildlife (the final count was 5 elk, 1 grizzly, 1 black bear, deer and plenty of squirrels), dipped our feet in glacier fed lakes, and ate s'mores by the fire.

I hope these journeys will keep my family close and instil in my children a lifelong love of road trips and adventure. I love to watch them laughing, bonding, and enjoying the great outdoors.

~ Alexa

Jeep

This is the beast we took to both Tofino and Banff. It fit 3 small children, 2 adults, and a mountain of supplies. We took it on highways, a ferry, and bumpy forest service roads. Well done Jeep.

Gary

Gary was chief child wrangler, chauffer, and key grip. He drove the Jeep, hauled the stuff, bribed the children, and was never at a loss for a joke. He constantly told Emily and I to 'block it out' when we stressed about knits... this wasn't helpful but it was funny! When I explained my plan to take 3 week old Bodhi on a camping trip he didn't bat an eye, he just said "let me book some campsites".

Hunter

Hunter loves a good road trip and she thought seeing wildlife up close was the coolest thing ever. Hunter doesn't always want to stand still, but she is an amazing little knitwear model for a 3-year-old.

Jones

Jones loves riding in the car. He never fusses and is hardly ever annoyed with the length of the journey. While he was a reluctant model at first, by the end we couldn't get the sweater off him!

Bodhi

Bodhi was brand spanking new on our Banff trip and she was the easiest baby in the world. She didn't mind being passed around bundled up in woolly sweaters on the chilly nights.

Emily (Emmy)

Emmy is many things to me: a great friend, a knitting companion, an auntie to my kids, and a model for Tin Can Knits. She performs each job with dedication and a sense of fun and adventure.

Jordan (Juju)

Hunter doesn't just call Jordan Juju, she has decided that 'Juju' is a classification of person, like uncle. Jordan drove all over the province, let me take his picture, and even dressed the way I asked. I couldn't ask for a better brother!

Alexa Ludeman ✦ Emily Wessel

YARNS

Thank you to the yarn companies and dyers who have contributed to this book. We appreciate your support and love working with your beautiful yarns.

Brooklyn Tweed
www.brooklyntweed.com

Cascade Yarns
www.cascadeyarns.com

Indigodragonfly
www.indigodragonfly.ca

Madelinetosh
www.madelinetosh.com

Sweet Fiber Yarns
www.sweetfiberyarns.com

SweetGeorgia Yarns
www.sweetgeorgiayarns.com

The Plucky Knitter
www.thepluckyknitter.com

THANKS

Road Trip wouldn't be possible without the folk who support us in the knitting community and in our personal lives.

- ✦ To our hundreds of test knitters - thanks for contributing your time and expertise.

- ✦ To Ashley, Emily and Marianela - thanks for knitting beautiful samples.

- ✦ To our tech editor Karen: thanks for your hard work, care, and attention to detail.

- ✦ To the lovely yarn shops that support us and carry our books: thanks for keeping us in business and inspiring us to continue designing and publishing patterns!

- ✦ Lastly, thanks to our partners, John and Gary, who put up with two pregnant ladies writing a book, and all the chaos that entails. Thanks for listening to our struggles and for being supportive and understanding as we created this book and our newest babies all at once.

ABOUT US

We are Alexa and Emily, the dynamic design duo behind Tin Can Knits. Alexa makes her home in Vancouver, Canada and Emily (born a Vancouver Island gal) now lives in Edinburgh, UK. Our business spans the Atlantic, but we are always on the same page when it comes to design!

While we each have our individual style, we find it inspiring to work together as a team. We love discussing everything from stitches to yarn choice, colours to photography, and everything in between.

At Tin Can Knits we create irresistible knits and offer outstanding pattern support. Check out our **website** and **blog** for in-depth tutorials covering techniques from basic cables to advanced lace design. Find us online where you can join the chat and tell us what you think.

www.tincanknits.com

other Tin Can Knits books :::